September–Decem

Day by Day
with
God

Rooting women's lives in the Bible

The Bible Reading Fellowship
Christina Press
Abingdon/Tunbridge Wells

The Bible Reading Fellowship
15 The Chambers, Vineyard
Abingdon OX14 3FE
brf.org.uk

The Bible Reading Fellowship (BRF) is a Registered Charity (233280)

ISBN 978 0 85746 616 7
All rights reserved

This edition © 2018 Christina Press and The Bible Reading Fellowship
Cover image © iStock

Distributed in Australia by:
MediaCom Education Inc, PO Box 610, Unley, SA 5061
Tel: 1 800 811 311 | admin@mediacom.org.au

Distributed in New Zealand by:
Scripture Union Wholesale, PO Box 760, Wellington
Tel: 04 385 0421 | suwholesale@clear.net.nz

Acknowledgements
Scripture quotations taken from The New Revised Standard Version of the Bible, Anglicised
edition, copyright © 1989, 1995 by the Division of Christian Education of the National Council of
the Churches of Christ in the United States of America. Used by permission. All rights reserved.
• Scripture quotations taken from The Holy Bible, New International Version (Anglicised edition)
copyright © 1979, 1984, 2011 by Biblica. Used by permission of Hodder & Stoughton Publishers, a
Hachette UK company. All rights reserved. 'NIV' is a registered trademark of Biblica. UK trademark
number 1448790. • Extracts from the Authorised Version of the Bible (The King James Bible), the
rights in which are vested in the Crown, are reproduced by permission of the Crown's Patentee,
Cambridge University Press. • Scripture quotations from the Contemporary English Version. New
Testament © American Bible Society 1991, 1992, 1995. Old Testament © American Bible Society
1995. Anglicisations © British & Foreign Bible Society 1996. Used by permission. • Scripture
taken from the Holy Bible, New International Reader's Version®. Copyright © 1996, 1998 Biblica.
All rights reserved throughout the world. Used by permission of Biblica. • Scripture quotations
taken from the Amplified® Bible (AMP). Copyright © 2015 by The Lockman Foundation. Used
by permission. www.Lockman.org. • Scripture quotations are taken from THE MESSAGE, copyright
© 1993, 1994, 1995, 1996, 2000, 2001, 2002 by Eugene H. Peterson. Used by permission of
NavPress. All rights reserved. Represented by Tyndale House Publishers, Inc. • Scripture taken
from the New King James Version®. Copyright © 1982 by Thomas Nelson. Used by permission.
All rights reserved. • The Living Bible copyright © 1971 by Tyndale House Foundation. Used by
permission of Tyndale House Publishers Inc., Carol Stream, Illinois 60188. All rights reserved.
• The New Testament in Modern English, Revised Edition, translated by J.B. Phillips, published
by HarperCollins Publishers Ltd. Copyright © 1958, 1960, 1972 by J.B. Phillips. • The Voice Bible
Copyright © 2012 Thomas Nelson, Inc. The Voice™ translation © 2012 Ecclesia Bible Society. All
rights reserved.

Every effort has been made to trace and contact copyright owners for material used in this
resource. We apologise for any inadvertent omissions or errors, and would ask those concerned
to contact us so that full acknowledgement can be made in the future.

A catalogue record for this book is available from the British Library

Printed by Gutenberg Press, Tarxien, Malta

Day by Day
with
God

Edited by **Ali Herbert** and **Jill Rattle**   September–December 2018

Writers in this issue

Sara Batts was a specialist librarian, and is now a curate in the East London part of the diocese of Chelmsford. Sara blogs at **www.sarabatts.co.uk**. She lives with a dog and hosts a cat.

Bridget Plass trained as an actress and has also worked as a secondary school teacher, residential social worker and a facilitator of women's groups. With her husband, Adrian, she performs as a speaker and entertainer, and she has written three books for BRF. Bridget and Adrian have four children.

Tracy Williamson is an author and speaker working for MBM Trust, a music and teaching ministry headed up by blind gospel singer Marilyn Baker. Tracy, who is deaf herself, has a golden labrador hearing dog called Goldie, and shares a home in Kent with Marilyn and her guide dog Saffie.

Jill Rattle is a retired secondary head teacher who lives in Birmingham with her husband. She is part of Gas Street Church, where she engages in prayer ministry and prison ministry. She co-edits *Day by Day with God*.

Christine Platt loves living in New Zealand. As well as engaging with local church ministry, she travels to East Timor regularly to teach English and the Bible.

Katy Jack is a wife, mother and lawyer. She juggles all the fun and ministry opportunities of being a school chaplain's wife, looking after her three sports-mad sons, being involved in their schools and clubs, coaching netball and working part time as an employment lawyer.

Anne Calver is a Baptist minister, author and speaker. Anne is passionate about God's word and Spirit, and seeing Jesus transform lives and release people's potential. She is married to Gavin and has two children, Amelie and Daniel.

Michele D. Morrison loves to write, and is working on a fourth book. She has been a regular contributor to *Woman Alive* and welcomes every opportunity to delve into scripture. Michele edits her church magazine, runs a small B&B, and blogs at **www.tearsamidthealiencorn.blogspot.com**.

Lyndall Bywater is a freelance writer, trainer and consultant in all things prayer. She lives in Canterbury with her husband.

Jean Watson has worked in teaching and editing, and her writing for children and adults has been published in books and magazines and broadcast on radio and TV. She has trained, and now works, as a spiritual director.

Jill Rattle and Ali Herbert write...

Jill: It's great to welcome new writers to *Day by Day with God* to join our familiar contributors. This issue opens with a beautiful set of notes from Book 1 of the Psalms by the Rev Dr Sara Batts. She has titled her notes: 'All human life is here: finding ourselves in the psalms'. While we human beings come in many shapes and sizes, with different gifts, experiences and backgrounds, we all experience the same range of emotions: hope, joy despair, anger, hatred, fear, worry, peace, turmoil, confusion, love – and many, many more. How wonderful, then, to come to the scriptures and find them all there and to discover that God understands how these emotions impact on us and on our relationship with him. We are often shaken by our negative emotions, but he is the immoveable 'rock' beneath us, keeping us safe.

We all have our mountain top and valley experiences, sometimes one following the other with unnerving rapidity – but Christine Platt shows us that the Lord is there in both, never leaving our side. And when we visit Daniel with Katy Jack, we know that this is true even in the most extreme of circumstances.

If only, through these readings, we could learn to trust him more for our own lives!

Ali: In between the mountain and the valley is that ordinary, everyday time which is where we spend the vast majority of our life. Do you have a favourite cup to have your morning tea in (I do!) or a particular way of loading the dishwasher? My dad always reloads the dishwasher the *right* way before switching it on – which is fortunate, because on one occasion my mum had carefully packed her iPad into the plate-stacking area!

We don't always think of these ordinary actions and items as great opportunities to pray, but in her fortnight of 'Praying the ordinary', Jill takes us through some ways of connecting with God in the most humdrum parts of our lives.

As we head together towards the 'mountain' experience of the Christmas season, we pray every blessing on you as you celebrate and think anew on the miracle of 'Immanuel', God with us.

All human life is here: finding ourselves in the psalms

Sara Batts writes:

Have you ever felt you're brimming over with thanks and joy? There's a psalm for that. Perhaps you feel anxious, afraid or doubtful? There's a psalm for that, too.

If we can't find the right words to express our feelings, the chances are we can find a psalm to do it on our behalf.

Over the next few days we will look at psalms from Book 1. The psalter – the book of Psalms – in the form we have it is split into five different books, each ending with words of praise. There are different ideas about how the psalter came to be, but it is generally accepted that psalms were collected and ordered for use in prayer and worship.

As a Church of England priest, I say several psalms a day in prayer. I find the words seep into my soul, giving me phrases and images to call to mind at other times. I love the sense that they have been used for centuries, that so many people before me have found the words to be helpful, inspiring, challenging and comforting.

Psalms show people being angry and desiring revenge. They show people being real and honest before God, not only in words of perfect praise: psalms even give us permission to shout at him!

I think sometimes there is an expectation that being a Christian means you have to be permanently happy in all kinds of adversity. The psalms can teach us not only how to praise, but also how to express sadness. The real world contains suffering and so does the psalter – there are many songs of lament.

The psalms of lament are like written permission from our forebears to question, giving us an outlet for our doubts and griefs. In this kind of psalm, we see praise and trust in God in spite of difficulties. Trust in God has not made the trouble go away, nor lessened its hurt. That is a reality we need to hold on to sometimes as we find our way through difficult times.

My prayer is that, as we look at praise, lament and everything in between, you will find new and rich ways to express your feelings before God.

Finding our way

They are like trees planted by streams of water, which yield their fruit in its season, and their leaves do not wither. (NRSV)

I've been counting 1 September as the first day of a new year for quite a long time now. So much of my life has been attuned to academic calendars that January's celebrations seem rather irrelevant. 1 September is when I review the year and make my resolutions for the months ahead. It seems fitting to begin our exploration of the psalms with Psalm 1, and its advice for life.

Psalm 1 contrasts the way of the wicked with the way of the righteous. Coming right at the start of the whole book of Psalms, it frames what is to come with thoughts on righteousness.

What a wonderful image we are given of a vigorous tree. A tree planted near, and refreshed by, a stream of water – able to grow and yield fruit.

If I resolved to be like that – refreshed, growing, yielding fruit – then my principal resolution would be to practise being in the presence of God. Everything else flows from that – how I spend my time, what my priorities are, etc.

If my New Year's resolutions are all about me, and not about God, then I've got my priorities wrong – which, after all, is what the first two commandments aim to put a stop to. For some of us, it might even be that we are doing so much in the service of God we're not paying attention to how – and if – we are being refreshed ourselves.

I wonder, too, how easy it is to slip into heeding the advice of the wicked. I wonder if the standards that a consumer society gives us, and we perhaps unknowingly follow, might lead us down the wrong path. Let's remember that we're priceless children of God, and seek our refreshment from his living water.

Lord, as I look to the month ahead, may I walk in your way in the days to come. Thank you for your life-giving Holy Spirit to guide and strengthen me.
SARA BATTS

Finding our safe place

In peace I will lie down and sleep, for you alone, Lord, make me dwell in safety. (NIV)

I sang this psalm with others several times a week during my ministry training, because it's part of the service of night prayer. I still find it hard to read it now without breaking into the chant, recalling the peace and beauty of the candle-lit chapel. Night prayer is designed to end the day quietly as we prepare for sleep.

Sleep is so very necessary to enable us to function. I recently acquired a puppy, and the broken nights in the first few weeks were exhausting. (My profound respect for parents of newborns has been redoubled!) Without sleep, we can't think straight and emotions are all over the place. I for one rarely choose fruit over chocolate on days I'm short on sleep. Lack of sleep has longer-term health effects, too. We need that rest!

While the end of the psalm points us to rest, the beginning shows us the psalmist in some distress. Psalm 4 is one of the many attributed to David, mirroring part of his story. The psalm takes us from this distress – the plea to be heard, the plea to be delivered from those who would mock – to the assurance of safety and rest in the Lord; an assurance that comes from knowing that the Lord will hear the prayer of the psalmist.

Oh, that it were so simple to be able to fall asleep when we're feeling assailed on many sides by worries! But perhaps we can take this psalm as an example of how to trust: how we can be assured that God is listening. God does care. Perhaps taking this assurance to heart is the ticket we need to a long, refreshing sleep.

Yes, the Lord is here. Yes, I can rejoice in his love for me, whatever may befall me. Yes, I can lie down and sleep, for the Lord will make me dwell in safety.

SARA BATTS

Finding our significance

When I look at your heavens, the work of your fingers, the moon and the stars that you have established; what are human beings that you are mindful of them, mortals that you care for them? (NRSV)

Living in East London, I can't really see the stars at night. There's so much light pollution, it's barely dark on the streets. When I am in the country-side and the wonder of the night sky is spread out above me, this psalm often comes to mind. The infinite beauty of the constellations rightly inspires awe; more so perhaps because we now see and know so much about the universe in which our fragile planet exists.

Before moving here, I used to pray for the world on my train commute, imagining a camera panning out from my seat to the carriage, then the whole train; then to all the trains going to my station; to the county, to Britain and to the world. All the while, noting how God knows and loves me, and how God knows and loves everyone else that comes into view as I zoom out. It helps give a sense of both perspective (I am one of 7.5 billion people) and grounding (God loves all those 7.5 billion, including me). There's something awe-inspiring in knowing I am significant despite my insignificance. I've just looked at a website with a counter ticking up, second by second, as babies are born. UNICEF reckons 353,000 new babies will arrive today.

Psalm 8 leads us in praise, rejoicing in this sense of awe and wonder that we are recognised by God and given status. It might be easy to think that if we have dominion over the world, we can do what we want. But there are 7.5 billion others sharing our home planet, and I think good stewardship of its resources is necessary so that all those born today will live a happy, healthy life.

Loving God, I thank you that you know me out of all the people on earth. I thank you that I am fearfully and wonderfully made in your image; that my name is on the palm of your hand.

SARA BATTS

Finding strength in lament

How long must I wrestle with my thoughts and day after day have sorrow in my heart? (NIV)

If you've ever been anxious and awake at 3.00 am, Psalm 13 is for you. This psalm has spoken to and for me during the most troubling times. I remember clearly the sense of relief at finding a psalm whose opening lines mirrored so well how I felt.

Psalm 13 is one of the shorter 'psalms of lament'. Lament means expressing sorrow or grief at a loss or change. I think that lament is a very under-used activity. It's a process which allows us to abandon the stiff upper lip; it allows us to be honest with God about our fears and difficulties; it is a framework on which we can hang our own difficult emotions; it is a process to take us from despair to trust.

In times of grief and stress, our thoughts may get stuck in an exhausting loop of 'If only' and 'What if?' We may wonder if God has forgotten us completely. If you find yourself in that place, often the hardest thing to do is to find new words to pray. Psalm 13 gives us those words, taking us on a journey from abandonment to a reminder of trust, and on to a declaration of praise. I like the idea of repeatedly reading this psalm. We focus on the lines that speak to us, stopping when we reach a sentiment we are not yet ready to own for ourselves. Gradually, perhaps weeks or months later, we find we can read a little further.

Perhaps the psalmist said these words through gritted teeth. Perhaps this is wanting to want to trust.

It is the legitimate voice of one who understands our despondency, our fear of neglect or our worry that our voice is unheard by God.

Is there anything in your life for which you would like to create the space and time to lament? God is ready and waiting to hear your prayer.

SARA BATTS

Finding our way in

O Lord, who may abide in your tent? Who may dwell on your holy hill? (NRSV)

As well as having psalms of prayer, praise and lament, the psalter also contains psalms that were used for specific liturgies in Jewish worship. It is easy to imagine Psalm 15 being recited at the gate to the temple in Jerusalem. 'Who can come in?' asks the priest. And worshippers respond, listing characteristics necessary for righteousness and for abiding in God's presence. It makes me think of the opening of the British parliament, with Black Rod banging on the door to the House of Commons after it's slammed in her face.

The response to the question is a good checklist of the way to be, even if it's easier to read the list than to live these virtues every day. Standing by our promises to others, even to our detriment, demands a strength of purpose. And are we always sure that we are not 'slandering with our tongues'? As James 3 reminds us, the tongue is tiny but can do great damage.

It may seem, then, that it would be impossible for anyone to come into God's presence, that the door will be closed to us, imperfect and unrighteous as we are. How wrong this is! No longer are we separated from God, kept to the outer courts of his temple. We have access to God through Jesus Christ and we are always welcome in God's presence. He wants to hear from us; he wants us to be in relationship with him. Instead of having to prove our righteousness in front of a heavy barricade, we're promised grace and a door that will open at the lightest of touches.

Pray today for those who are persecuted, whose worship and prayer must be held secretly for fear of violence and reprisals.

SARA BATTS

Finding our confidence

My God, my God, why have you forsaken me? Why are you so far from helping me, from the words of my groaning? (NRSV)

I struggle sometimes with people who expect me to be constantly happy because I am a Christian, and even more so because I am a minister. Yes, I know the love of God; yes, I look forward to heaven where all my questions will be resolved; yes, I am called to serve him joyfully. Yet, equally, I live in the world and I see its problems – which can be upsetting. I am not immune either from personal sorrow or the feeling that God isn't listening.

Psalm 22 is probably familiar to us all from the Easter readings. Jesus' cry of abandonment from upon the cross comes from the opening line. Jesus immersed himself in the psalms and found the words spoke for him in his agony. The casting of lots for his clothing (v. 18) and the cries to 'save yourself' (vv. 7–8) are all foreseen in Psalm 22.

Jesus knew this psalm. We share the book of Psalms – the prayer book of the Bible – with him. However, our difficulties and troubles are a long way from brutal crucifixion.

These psalms allow us to appreciate that not all is plain sailing, but that complaint and lament can be tied up with praise and confidence. In fact, we lament *because* we can be confident that God hears us.

And so we can be confident of the deliverance from trouble that the psalmist proclaims and that Jesus knew, too. We may have to wait longer than the third day for resolution – it might be a lifetime's work of prayer and waiting.

In response, we have a duty to praise and glorify our Lord; we should stand in awe of his might; we should tell our brothers and sisters of his love.

Lord Jesus, you knew the pain of loss and abandonment. Hear me when I cry out to you. Console and strengthen me in my times of difficulty and rejoice with me in my praise.

SARA BATTS

Finding our rest

He makes me lie down in green pastures; he leads me beside still waters; he restores my soul. (NRSV)

How do you feel, reading Psalm 23? Does it bring back memories of funerals? Or singing at school? Is it very familiar? Whatever our initial reaction, let's read it today noticing that the green pastures and still waters come *before* the refreshing of our souls.

As a brand-new curate, I wanted to change the world. My sense of self-worth was tied up with the length of my to-do list. I wanted to prove myself by being busy and needed. Paying attention to how my body felt was the last thing on the list. I was too busy being busy to prioritise sleep or exercise, despite knowing how good running made me feel. I was grazing in the wrong place.

I think here, too, of friends with chronic illnesses whose attention is called daily to their physical well-being. For these friends, rest is enforced and unwelcome. Being over-busy and under-busy are both challenging states to be in. Both have a restlessness at their heart.

Psalm 23 is where we can go to meditate on this restlessness being soothed. We see again the image of water (the Spirit) to quench our thirst and to allow us to flourish – like the trees in Psalm 1.

Sheep, I am told, nibble themselves lost. A new patch here, another a few paces away – and, in time, they're a long way from home. I think busyness can be like that – just one more task, then another – and before we know it we've lost sight of the reason we're busy in the first place. The 'doing' for God takes over from 'being' for God. Can we allow ourselves to be led back to the still waters? To put aside the busyness – or accept the enforced rest – and find our still centre in God?

Try today to sit still and take some long, deep breaths. Without judging yourself, note how your body feels. Thank God for his amazing creation – including in our own bones and muscles.

SARA BATTS

Finding our voice to praise

O magnify the Lord with me, and let us exalt his name together. (NRSV)

What a wonderful psalm of praise! A sense of joyfulness and thankfulness abounds in this song , thought to refer to David's escape by feigning madness (1 Samuel 21:10–15).

We have, in the last few days, looked at psalms that express worry, anxiety and abandonment. I wanted to finish these studies in the psalms with joyful praise to the Lord. Just as we can own the words of those earlier psalms for our difficult times, we can adopt as our own these phrases of praise, too.

We might not need to physically escape from our surroundings, but life for all of us has its share of troubles and fears. There are all kinds of issues that we might name, be they family worries, finances or problems at work. God wants us to take these problems to him. He is ready and waiting and willing to listen to our outpourings.

The challenge for us as Christians is to trust and to praise God, even when we are in the midst of the issues. It takes great faith to take these words and make them our own if we are in the middle of a difficult situation. It takes faith and it takes practice and strength from the Holy Spirit to be able to praise in all circumstances.

Praising the God who loves and guides us is a natural response to knowing that we are safe with him and loved by him: thanksgiving that leads to action – in the case of this psalm, the overflowing willingness to teach others the way of life. Fear of the Lord isn't trembling in terror before him. It's more like a 'true reverence' – not terror, but the sense of awe that God deserves.

Let's make this our song of praise today: 'I will bless the Lord at all times; his praise shall continually be in my mouth.'

SARA BATTS

Our creative God and his creative children

Bridget Plass writes:

'Oh, she's very creative' is often intended as a compliment, but in some people's minds, this relegates our talents to only being good at papercraft or cake-icing. It is certainly great to be good at these things – but creativity is so much wider than just this. Sarah Corbett, founder of Craftivist Collective, talks of how crafting can bring together 'hands, heart and head'; but, more than that, combining craft with activism can dramatically impact our world.

My own experience of being involved with communal creativity is that it leaves me a lot of room for 'mouth'; chatting while doing something is a favourite pastime. On the other hand, I'm aware that for some people the opposite is true, and that being creative for them requires quietness and solitude, where the imagination can doodle dreams while the hands play with paint or words or music. But can 'being creative' mean even more than that for us, God's children?

Through these notes, we are going to look at different aspects of our creator and how they can affect our lives. This triune God didn't simply create an extraordinary natural world, but also popped in extras for all of us, so we can be part of the creative process, with gifts of imagination, ability to respond to beauty and… thinking. Our Father God loves to receive his children's amateur (or not!) contributions and listen to their ideas and their dreams; the Holy Spirit hovered over the waters before the world came into being and his ingenuity can stir within us; and Jesus' creativity showed through every encounter and in every story, and his heart went out to all he met.

The creative power of response

In the beginning God created the heaven and the earth… and darkness was upon the face of the deep. And the Spirit of God moved upon the face of the waters. (KJV)

'The Spirit of God All-Powerful gave me the breath of life' (Job 33:4, CEV). Isn't it hugely reassuring that the Holy Spirit was energising creation from the beginning? Genesis tells us that 'God created' and that his Spirit 'moved'. The same Spirit that breathed life into Adam energises us still. Generous-to-a-fault God continues to pop into us seeds of imagination, creativity, dreams and, best of all, the ability to respond to the diversity and splendour of creation. Without our emotional response, all this would be reduced to the utilitarian, the biological and the geographical. Splashing in puddles may not seem quite the miracle it did when we were wellie-clad four-year-olds, but when storms rage or waves crash against breakwaters or explode over man-made barriers, we shiver in awe. When our senses are assaulted by the heady scent of roses or we crinkle the same noses in disgust at the smell of manure, we are similarly involved. In our creative response, we hear the heartbeat of our creator.

In 2016, Adrian and I spent two months surviving the scalding Australian heat. The highlight of our working tour was a Sunday spent in a rainforest high above the sweltering plains of northern Queensland, watching with utter delight dozens of platypuses playing in the cool sheltered waters of Eungella National Park. How our triune God must have enjoyed creating the platypus puzzle! In our delighted response, something deep within us relaxed. We weren't in church. We weren't ministering, working, trying hard or actively worshipping. We were simply being, and we both felt closer to the creator of the universe than we had for a long time. Everything fell into place and it was all okay.

To encourage us all: Philip Yancey tells how he almost lost his faith through a formal Christian upbringing, only to be drawn back through romantic love, classical music and the beauty of the natural world.

BRIDGET PLASS

Where does creativity spring from?

So if anyone is in Christ, there is a new creation: everything old has passed away; see, everything has become new! (NRSV)

'He put a new song in my mouth, a hymn of praise to our God' (Psalm 40:3, NIV). What do we mean when we talk about 'creativity'? One interesting definition suggests a work of creation is something 'new, intentional and valuable'. Paintings by Bubbles, Michael Jackson's pet chimp, sell for over £500 each and clearly have a value to his fans, but do they fit the criteria of an intentional creation? Are they inspired? Do they spring from the desire to express feelings or ideas? Does this matter? I'm not sure, but I do know that creativity does not seem to be a humanly generated power.

In the 1970s, there was an explosion of the work of the Holy Spirit which had a profound effect on worship music. It didn't arise from a desire to be 'cool' or relevant to young people. It was God, creating something new, intentional and valuable to resource his beloved church. Graham Kendrick, already an established singer songwriter, was by his own admission still inhibited by conventions in church music. One day, he felt 'something tangible happening… the Spirit urging me, and overflowing with something I knew didn't come from me'. His songs became richer, his understanding deepened and he was joined by many equally inspired musicians. Guitars, drums and rhythm entered our churches.

So far, so very good. The danger nowadays is that as soon as something genuinely new is born, we are able to clone it, to reproduce it, falling into the danger of diluting the very thing we are trying to bottle! Now, if a church can't pull together a worship band, perhaps they feel they're failing. And do we really want to hear another song with the same tempo, similar words and chords as every other worship song? Sparkling water is wonderful. What can we do to ensure that it doesn't become stagnant?

Dear Father, help us to drink constantly from the original spring of your creative Holy Spirit so that all we create in your name will bring health and encouragement to your world.

BRIDGET PLASS

A child's-eye view

Jesus said, 'Let the children come to me, and don't try to stop them! People who are like these children belong to God's kingdom.' (CEV)

When my mother died, I found a cardboard box stuffed with treasures, among them a small square of bright purple satin cloth, the raw edges adorned with huge clumsy stitches and, bang in the middle, a stagger-ingly large red button. I recognised it. Despite all evidence to the contrary, it was a handkerchief and, to my five-year-old critical eye, a masterpiece. Those of us with children or godchildren may have been presented with portraits displaying a huge oval body complete with buttons, a wide wobbly smile and one blob eye. We will know from the shiny pride with which the painting is presented that, in the imagination of the small creator, our unique beauty has been faithfully captured!

Their critical eye will hopefully develop along with their motor skills, but there is a danger that, as adults, we begin to limit imagination, look-ing at what we create and dismissing it as imperfect. In our church com-munities, do we maybe worry too much about how our efforts will be judged by the world? Do we try so hard to present such a perfect image of Christianity that we stifle the very creativity we hoped to encourage? Children have no problem with the concept of heaven, easily imagining a world where people never die, where nobody goes hungry and the lion literally lies down with the lamb. Naïve? Childish? Or open to the truth of the kingdom – the way of flexibility, freedom, wonder and imagination? C.S. Lewis said, 'Even in Literature and Art, no man who bothers about originality will ever be original; whereas if you simply try to tell the truth (without caring two pence how often it has been told before) you will, nine times out of ten, become original without ever having noticed it' (*Mere Christianity*, 1952).

Father God, help me to go back to the time when everything I heard about your kingdom was fresh, new and exciting, and I knew the truth glowed. Help me to find a way to share that.

BRIDGET PLASS

Thinking outside the box

'All of life is far more boring than words could ever say. Our eyes and our ears are never satisfied with what we see and hear. Everything that happens has happened before; nothing is new, nothing under the sun.' (CEV)

Not all of us are called to be 'primary creators', but we, too, can be part of the creative process. One of my favourite cartoons first appeared in *The New Yorker*. A harassed owner is speaking to his cat while firmly pointing out the litter tray on the floor. 'I never, ever, want you to think outside the box' is the caption. 'Thinking outside the box' is used to describe creative thinking, but what does that mean? Well, for starters, it doesn't mean discarding the box!

When I was in Zambia many years ago, I attended a wonderful carnival day where impromptu group dances were a glorious feature. 'They don't even have to work at it, do they?' I remarked to our guide. 'It just comes naturally.' He smilingly pointed out a line of barefoot small children, concentration etched on to their faces as they swayed and clicked their hips, inexpertly copying the movements of the exuberant chain of adult dancers. True, we may feel there is nothing new under the sun, but we, like the Zambian children, are following an expert capable of creating new steps to the familiar dance.

When challenged by those who thought they had caught him, Jesus didn't trash the box of the law; he just gracefully leapt outside of it. 'Let anyone among you who is without sin be the first to throw a stone' (John 8:7, NRSV). 'Give back to Caesar what is Caesar's and to God what is God's' (Mark 12:17, NIV). 'The Sabbath was made for man, not man for the Sabbath' (Mark 2:27, NRSV).

As God's children, maybe we, too, can approach familiar situations afresh, and, after learning the steps, breathe new life into the dried-up bones of thinking, speaking and doing, and, without discarding the box, create something fresh and new – a genuine 'fresh expression'.

Dear Father, help us not to despise what has gone before, but teach us new steps and give us the courage to follow you wherever you lead us.

BRIDGET PLASS

19

The fermentation process

'Why do the followers of John and those of the Pharisees often go without eating, while your disciples never do?'... Jesus answered, 'No one pours new wine into old wineskins. The wine would swell and burst the old skins... New wine must be put into new wineskins.' (CEV)

It's so easy to think of creativity as something that leaps spontaneously and effortlessly from the soul. Yet we know that many of our greatest painters learned their craft by being apprenticed to an established artist, under stern control until the moment when their signature style broke free, exploding into their masterpiece. The painstaking learning of any craft could be likened to a fermentation process. Many well-respected actors, poets, principal dancers and our greatest composers are living proof of this. But should we associate creativity solely with the years of hard graft, culminating in a burst of sublime artistic expression?

Actually, we see creativity clearly when we look at exploration, scientific discovery and sport. 'One small step for mankind,' announced the man at the pinnacle of years of space exploration. Dick Fosbury perfected the high-jump technique that was to astonish the world after endless practice within accepted norms. Many of our most innovative scientists stood on the shoulders of those who had come before. Marie Curie is famous for isolating radium, an achievement that would eventually revolutionise cancer treatment, but she and her husband Pierre built on years of work by other scientists.

As I said yesterday, Jesus didn't trash the box or platform of the old existing law. He came to fulfil it, standing on it as if it were a gnarled old soap box, to shout the good news of a fresh and freer way. He always gave credit to the years of hard slog put in by John the Baptist who, through a life of self-sacrifice, had initiated the process of fermentation that would allow the old wine skins to eventually be cast aside and fresh ones prepared for the new wine of the kingdom.

'This is what the past is for! Every experience God gives us, every person he puts in our lives is the perfect preparation for the future that only he can see' (Corrie ten Boom, The Hiding Place, *1971).*

BRIDGET PLASS

Painting with light

He wants me to help those in Zion who are filled with sorrow. I will put beautiful crowns on their heads in place of ashes... [and] give them a spirit of praise in place of a spirit of sadness. They will be like oak trees that are strong and straight. The Lord himself will plant them. (NIRV)

As a child, I was definitely not gifted at art, and I remember my joy in being given a magic painting book. All I had to do was fill my fat brush with water, apply said brush, and the black and white picture sprang into magical colour. Well, the magic maybe overtook the quality of the colours, but I was incredibly impressed by my artistic achievement. Of course, I now know that the coloured dots were already there and I was merely bringing them to life.

Kenneth Williams, a photographer, claimed in the iconic *Hancock's Half Hour*, 'I paint with light.' We follow a man who painted with light, transfiguring the black and white lives of those he met, a revelation of their true colours. Love is good at that.

Actually, love can be too creative at the beginning of a relationship. Like filters applied to a photograph, human first love can remove blemishes and create a perfect but distorted image. As we know, Jesus sees our blemishes, but his divine filter imaginatively penetrates the flawed exterior to reveal the more colourful truth of who we were created to be.

The paintbrush of the Master, loaded with love and light, heals and restores. It enabled the woman taken in adultery to believe she could change her life; it inspired Zacchaeus to be a warmer version of himself; and it even enabled Peter to believe he was forgiven.

Of course, we can never emulate Jesus, and we may not excel as artists, but maybe we, too, can paint with light, fill our 'life brush' with imagination, love and hope, create beauty from ugliness and bring colour magically out of drabness.

Remind us, Father, that everyone has coloured dots inside them. Help us to paint with your light and love.

BRIDGET PLASS

Created in his image

God said, 'Now we will make humans, and they will be like us. We will let them rule the fish, the birds, and all other living creatures.' (CEV)

Whatever our attitude to the Genesis creation story, one thing is clear throughout God's story as told in the Bible: we are supposed to be like the God we worship, and therefore carry a huge responsibility towards the world loved into being by the Trinity. Yet, for many of us, especially those who live in urban environments, that relationship isn't even a memory. This was brought into focus for me this year when my son Joe, working in Nairobi, took a group of orphans from one of the city's sprawling slums on a budget safari where, wide-eyed, they saw for the first time the animals for which their country is famous.

A clear image of what God hoped we would be is found in the ancient spirituality of the Australian aborigines, who had a close kinship with their environment. Believing this relationship to be fundamental, they established ways in which all things were interconnected so as to maintain order and sustainability. In the area where they lived, each tribe had the stewardship of the flora or fauna which could not be eaten, and which survived without being plundered to extinction. Being nomadic, each tribe would move on a regular basis to another area where, again, the physical resources of their new home would be preserved. They had a sense of the 'sacredness' of the created world.

Rebuilding our relationship with the created world may seem an impossible task, as we helplessly watch the demise of the rainforest and the melting of the ice floe. But maybe we can all find a way to engage with, love and respect the needs of our planet – after all, we are created in God's own image.

'The earth is the Lord's and all that is in it' (Psalm 24:1, NRSV).

'The groves were God's first temples. Ere man learned to hew the shaft, and lay the architrave… He knelt down, And offered to the Mightiest solemn thanks And supplication' (William Cullen Bryant, 1794–1878).

BRIDGET PLASS

1 and 2 Timothy

Tracy Williamson writes:

In my 30 plus years of working with blind singer songwriter Marilyn Baker, I've had many interesting experiences. One was accompanying Marilyn to various music studios as she recorded her albums. As a deaf person, I felt like a fish out of water in this environment of singers, musicians, instruments, cables, mixers, producers, ecstasy, frustration and joy. I was always drawn into the almost tangible exhilaration in the atmosphere, but what amazed me was the juxtaposition of passionate music with the necessary exactitude of using the right cable or turning a knob. To create perfect songs, there had to be a combination of beauty and passion with detailed care and action.

As we ponder Paul's two letters to Timothy, we will find a similar pattern of detail running throughout. Paul is not looking to create a music album but, far more importantly, to develop a special partnership and a great leader. Juxtaposed we'll see Paul's thankfulness to God for his salvation, fatherly belief in Timothy, hatred of all that corrupts the gospel and passionate commitment to taking that gospel to all. More than Paul's other letters, these two are personal, and through them we see not only Paul's heart but glimpses of Timothy's – and glimpses of ourselves, too.

What does God want to say to us through these letters? As I reflect on what to glean for our notes, I feel both encouraged and challenged. These letters are part of the Bible for a reason: that we all, not just Timothy, become empowered to grow in our calling; that we all see the corruption of faith and lifestyle in our society, in our churches or even in our own hearts, and as a result are convicted to pray.

As we see Timothy struggling with anxieties, will we recognise the fears holding us back, too? When Paul affirms Timothy's calling as a leader, do we need assurance in our calling as well? We may cringe at Paul's words about women, but don't dismiss them – there are dynamic truths, comfort and challenge to draw from every section.

God gives Paul a clear vision of the future – showing that we, not just Timothy, are called to be in partnership with him. Will we rise up to that and take on the baton, with Paul's joyful assurance in our hearts that we are working towards a holy crown and eternal inheritance?

Be encouraged and empowered.

Rooted in truth

Paul, an apostle of Christ Jesus by the command of God our Saviour, and of Christ Jesus our hope. To Timothy my true son in the faith: grace, mercy and peace from God the Father and Christ Jesus our Lord. (NIV)

Being intrinsically nosy, I love that we are privy here to Paul's conversation with his great friend, Timothy. As with social media today, we see a glimpse of what really matters to Paul. He wants to help Timothy grow in his leadership and not get sucked in to the trends of other leaders who are 'devoting themselves to myths and endless genealogies'. Fashions and cultures change, but this tendency to get together in little cliques and air our views as if they're the only answer is just as true today as it was then.

But Paul wants to root Timothy in foundational truth and this is equally vital for us. Paul knows God as his loving Father who has shaped his personality and who, through Jesus, has forgiven and equipped him for his destiny. He begins his letter by confidently writing: 'Paul, an apostle of Christ Jesus by the command of God'. In the flow of this confidence, Paul then confers true identity on Timothy, saying he is 'my true son in the faith'. Paul releases God's grace, mercy and peace over Timothy so that he can lead his churches effectively.

We all need such rooting to live as God's beloved children overflowing with his grace and powerfully drawing others into his love. We are all called to this, even though we will not all be leaders. How do we respond when people are talking negatively? Do we get sucked in or are we channels of hope and truth?

The first time I heard God I was mired in emotional pain, but he said I was his daughter and he would never abandon me. That beautiful word became a heart-foundation, empowering me to reach out to many others.

He wants to do the same through you.

Are you living out of God's grace, mercy and peace or out of negative judgements? Prayerfully give to God everything unhelpful you've come to believe and ask him to ground you afresh as his beloved child.

TRACY WILLIAMSON

The wonder of his grace

I was shown mercy so that in me, the worst of sinners, Christ Jesus might display his immense patience as an example for those who would believe in him and receive eternal life. Now to the King eternal, immortal, invisible, the only God, be honour and glory for ever and ever. Amen. (NIV)

Today, I have a deep sense of some readers' pain: that you feel a failure and can't forgive yourself. When you look back, you are crippled with regret. You believe you have no right to live in forgiveness and joy.

God loves you and wants to minister his forgiveness to you today. In this passage, Paul is also looking back and knows: 'I was once a blasphemer and a persecutor and a violent man.' He describes himself as the worst of sinners, yet there is no sense of crippling shame. This is because, even while he faces his sin, his focus is on Jesus' mercy: 'Christ Jesus came into the world to save sinners.'

He goes on to say that, through Christ showing him such love, others would be given an amazing example of how real Christ's gifts of forgiveness and eternal life are. God wants us all to be able to share this testimony. Maybe you feel that the things you've done are so bad that you can't be forgiven? But Christ's mercy is so much greater. Paul understands this and it's why he erupts in joyful praise and worship.

Paul also encourages Timothy to believe and live out God's prophetic words. I once had to choose to believe that God's words to me would be good. My mind was full of all the mocking words I'd grown up with, which felt true but were lies. Would God be any different? Paul told Timothy he would 'fight the good fight' as he followed God's words which strengthen and empower. I chose to trust in God's truth, and Satan's power over me has been broken step by step. God loves to speak, to transform and guide us. Choose to believe his loving words to you today.

'The Spirit you received does not make you slaves, so that you live in fear again; rather, the Spirit you received brought about your adoption to sonship. And by him we cry, "Abba, Father"' (Romans 8:15, NIV).

TRACY WILLIAMSON

What is your vision?

I urge, then, first of all, that petitions, prayers, intercession and thanksgiving be made for all people – for kings and all those in authority, that we may live peaceful and quiet lives in all godliness and holiness. This is good, and pleases God our Saviour, who wants all people to be saved and to come to a knowledge of the truth. (NIV)

Society pushes us to fulfil our destiny, and spiritually, too, we are taught to seek God for personal vision. I believe that vision is key to living motivated and effective lives; but, beyond that, God wants us to commit to his vision of making his kingdom of love and mercy known in our world.

Paul is giving us some keys to living godly lives. Firstly, he encourages all of us to pray – for everyone! How is your prayer life? Mine is not great. I pray if I feel burdened by a particular situation, but soon stop once the crisis has passed. But do we understand how powerful ongoing prayer for our world is? It releases an atmosphere of godliness, holiness and the very pleasure of God. God's vision is that all may be saved and come to know him, and he has chosen you to be part of that. As this letter shows, prayer is vital.

Do you feel that you don't have much to offer? Your value to God is nothing to do with popularity or success. All God wants is for you to pray his prayers and reach out with his love in your own unique way.

Sometimes I feel socially inadequate because of my deafness and try to hide behind looking good or achievements. Maybe you feel inadequate? Don't strive to be noticed, for you already display God's beauty with your 'good deeds', as Paul puts it. God told me once that I was more beautiful to him than everything else he'd made. I'd felt more like a blade of grass than a beautiful flower or majestic mountain, but this word now motivates my prayers and actions, for I long for others to understand his amazing love and unique delight in them, too.

Thank you, Father, that you've chosen me to be part of your vision to reach this world with your love. Please help me to pray today and do something for someone that will reveal the beauty of your love.

TRACY WILLIAMSON

Household management

He must manage his own family well and see that his children obey him, and he must do so in a manner worthy of full respect. (If anyone does not know how to manage his own family, how can he take care of God's church?) (NIV)

Recently I asked a lady in church, 'What do you do?'

'Nothing,' she said, 'I'm just a mum.'

I felt sad that there are those who think bringing up children and creating a home are of little importance, when in God's eyes they are vital.

This chapter emphasises the importance of our lives as a whole, not just the so-called spiritual things like leading a house group or preaching. Our gentleness, integrity at work and at home and ability to command our children's respect: these are qualities God looks for in his leaders.

Reflect for a moment: do you know that God is always with you and loves all that you put into your home and your relationships? Is it through your responses that his love is made known in your family and friends? Could your efforts to resolve conflicts or be more patient at home equip you to help struggling people in your church?

What do your private attitudes reveal about you? I am in itinerant ministry and often publicly share my testimony, sometimes while still feeling resentful towards someone I know. Far more authentic are the times I welcome someone into my home or react well to criticism. Is God's love revealed through your quoting a Bible verse or through your patience when your friends or children drive you mad?

Be encouraged; all you do unobtrusively for the people in your life causes you to grow more like Jesus. Never dismiss yourself as unimportant, for as you build your home and relationships, you are also building the kingdom of God, and he will bless and use you more and more.

Persevere

Do not neglect your gift, which was given you through prophecy when the body of elders laid their hands on you. Be diligent in these matters; give yourself wholly to them, so that everyone may see your progress. Watch your life and doctrine closely. Persevere. (NIV)

Do you need encouraging today? Perhaps you feel inadequate or some-one has been disparaging. Paul encouraged Timothy not just to keep going, but to keep believing in what God made him to be. He tells him to 'have nothing to do with godless myths and old wives' tales'.

What we listen to is so important. Are you allowing others' negative opinions to colour your view of yourself or God? Paul says that some will follow deceiving spirits, and their teaching will be full of rules and restrictions. But Jesus died to free us from all that and live lives of joy and peace. Paul says the devil is behind these deceptions, but that we need to focus on becoming godly as 'godliness has value for all things, holding promise for both the present life and the life to come'.

Are you panicking at the call to 'godliness'? But true godliness is free-dom, thanksgiving, hope and intimacy with the God who loves you. God says, 'I love you and want to speak my words into your heart.' Paul tells Timothy, 'Don't let anyone look down on you because you are young,' and encourages him not to neglect his gift.

We can so easily become discouraged. Some years ago, believing it was of God, I went for ordination selection but was rejected. My con-fidence took such a knock that I virtually gave up writing and stopped expecting to be given prophecies, which had previously been a source of blessing to others. That deception lasted for years until I accepted that God still wanted to use me, just not through ordination. Now I am writing again and listening to him for blessings for others. This time, I will perse-vere and diligently search my heart to be sure I'm not being deceived by the enemy's lies.

Integrity

Do not rebuke an older man harshly, but exhort him as if he were your father. Treat younger men as brothers, older women as mothers and younger women as sisters with absolute purity. Give proper recognition to those widows who are really in need. (NIV)

Will my epitaph say that I was a woman of integrity, whose faith was evident by the genuineness of my love?

Paul shows in this chapter how such godly qualities are central to our calling. To have integrity: to not gossip, show partiality or believe accusations, but rather to love those around us like family. That is our real calling. Will I view the taciturn treasurer as my father or that irritating lady as my sister? Do I care for that lonely widowed lady as my mother? This is how God loves us, so nothing is more important than us loving others in the same way.

I was really impacted by God's love after becoming a Christian. I was a mess because of years of abuse. One night, I knocked on the door of a couple in my church. We didn't know each other well, it was after midnight and they had young children. I was crying, soaking wet and exhausted. They simply loved me: hot drink, bed, hot water bottle, no questions, no judgements. My life began to turn around from that moment. There is nothing more powerful than loving others as God loves us.

Are you lonely or hurt by family? Be comforted, for God cares and wants to help you. Paul challenges us to care for the widows in our families and deal wisely with our own loneliness. Are we wasting time pursuing unhealthy habits? If I am down, I often escape into inward things like Facebook but, like Timothy, we are called to look outward, to be a true friend to those around us and seek to have supportive not destructive relationships. God is looking for genuine integrity and gentleness as we deal with life's messy situations.

Thank you, Lord, that you care about my life, who I am, what I think and how I respond to others. Please give me your ability to love them as you love me, and help me become a real person of integrity.

TRACY WILLIAMSON

Take hold

Pursue righteousness, godliness, faith, love, endurance and gentleness… Take hold of the eternal life to which you were called… Command them to do good, to be rich in good deeds, and to be generous… They will lay up treasure for themselves as a firm foundation… [and] take hold of the life that is truly life. (NIV)

This is a powerful chapter full of words like flee, pursue, fight, take hold and guard! Such active words show we can't sit back, expecting God to do everything, for we are partners with him in pursuing his righteousness. A lady once said: 'God's had years to change me, so why hasn't he done it?' She wanted change to just happen; but we partner with him, deliberately taking hold of his truth, fleeing from negatives, guarding our hearts.

Paul is speaking about the kind of passions that fuel our lives. Godliness with contentment is the right kind. The deep-heart contentment of knowing we are unconditionally loved gives birth to the passionate pursuit of kingdom qualities like faith, love and gentleness. Such passion is wonderful, as it empowers us to do amazing things for him; but Paul is keen that we don't get hooked into the wrong passions. He describes 'the love of money' as being the root of all kinds of evil. Money is a necessity and can be used for great good, but if our passion is just to get rich and powerful, we are on a dangerous path. When on walks with my dogs, I may call them, but if they've spotted something more exciting they'll pursue it with absolute dedication until they've taken hold (or mouth) of it, sometimes with disastrous results!

Do you think, 'I'm a Christian, these things won't affect me'? But such striving is engrained in our culture and churches, so Paul instructs us to consciously 'take hold of the life that is truly life'. To me, nothing equals knowing God or the joy of seeing others experience his love. It makes me long to be part of all he is doing in our broken world. Will we take hold of that passion today?

Loving Father, thank you that you've set me on an exhilarating path. Forgive me for chasing after things that don't matter and help me to live in contentment. I take hold of your amazing love for me today.

TRACY WILLIAMSON

Not ashamed

So do not be ashamed of the testimony about our Lord or of me his prisoner. Rather, join with me in suffering for the gospel, by the power of God. He has saved us and called us to a holy life. (NIV)

I love Facebook, but lots of my posts have Christian themes, while many of my Facebook friends are not Christians. What must they think of all my references to praying or being thankful? I know I am bearing witness, but sometimes I feel embarrassed.

Paul highlights this when he says 'do not be ashamed' and 'this is no cause for shame'. Paul challenges us to pursue God, but embarrassment and shame restrict us from that purpose.

Do you struggle with testifying or feel shame about a weakness in your life? God has shown me I am afraid of looking a fool. He said, 'You always want people's affirmation because you fear being different, but won't you let my love wash those false fears away?'

Paul urges Timothy to live full-on for God, fanning into flame his God-given gift, because 'the Spirit God gave us does not make us timid, but gives us power, love and self-discipline'. This is true for us all.

Maybe, like me, you hold back or have a weakness like Paul's chains that make you feel you're not a good witness? I was told as a new Christian that I had to accept that God could not use me as a deaf person. I felt so condemned. But those words were a lie, the kind of idle talk that Paul tells Timothy to avoid at all costs.

We all suffer in different ways but God says, 'Don't draw back, but love me with the whole of who you are even in your weakness.' In his hands, our weaknesses become wonderful reflections of his grace. As Paul says: 'This is no cause for shame, because I know whom I have believed, and am convinced that he is able to guard what I have entrusted to him until that day.'

Forgive me, Lord, for being embarrassed to talk about you and ashamed of my weaknesses. You are so full of love. Thank you for choosing me and your amazing gifts. Please help me live full-on for you.

TRACY WILLIAMSON

For the sake of...

Therefore I am ready to persevere and stand my ground with patience and endure everything for the sake of the elect so that they too may obtain the salvation which is in Christ Jesus with the reward of eternal glory. (AMPC)

For whose sake do we act? I enjoy relaxing in a bath; I also walk my dogs regularly. The bath is for my own sake; the walks, primarily for the dogs. Everything we do has an effect, either on ourselves or others. It is wise to think of our own needs, because God hasn't called us to be wrung out, but beyond self-awareness is the call to live for 'God's sake'. This is not always easy, yet is wonderfully joy-giving.

Paul declares that he will 'endure everything for the sake of the elect that they too may obtain salvation'. That 'everything' includes his present suffering. The love of Jesus has so impacted Paul's heart that his circumstances matter less to him than those who need to hear the gospel. He is totally living 'for their sake'.

It's not likely we'll face prison like Paul, but there is always some cost – things like our time and money may need sacrificing. So Paul urges Timothy to 'be strong in the grace that is in Christ Jesus' and also to 'endure like a good soldier'. His grace – that is, his love, favour, forgiveness and gifts – fills our hearts, so that we long to love as he loves.

Onesiphorus lovingly served Paul, who was deeply helped and inspired to give back by interceding for Onesiphorus and his family. Blessing others always has a domino effect. We can live miserably, thinking no one cares, or we can reach out in God's love and see his power released.

You are part of this caring culture that God is creating. Paul urges Timothy to entrust his teachings to others so that God's love will impact more and more. Will we, too, speak and act – for their sakes?

Ask the Lord to remind you of when someone has lovingly served you. Thank him for his love and ask how you can now bless them. Act upon what comes to you.

TRACY WILLIAMSON

Present yourself to God as one approved

Warn them before God against quarrelling about words; it is of no value and only ruins those who listen. Do your best to present yourself to God as one approved, a worker who does not need to be ashamed and who correctly handles the word of truth. (NIV)

These letters share issues that weigh heavily on Paul, one of them being 'quarrelling about words'. Why does Paul hate quarrelling and godless chatter? Paul says it will infect and 'spread like gangrene', a sobering description with its connotation of death, here the death of true faith. As Paul is in prison for sharing the gospel, it's not surprising he feels passionate about the destruction wrought by careless talk and wants to impart that passion to us.

Paul also urges us: 'Do your best to present yourself to God as one approved.' Do you know that you are chosen and approved by God and have no need to be ashamed? Paul wants this truth to transform us.

Recently, I was praying about how I waste time when doing something important. I often fall asleep or get distracted, then feel condemned for not giving the job my best. As I prayed, I suddenly remembered times when I'd been told I wasn't good enough. A lie of inferiority had imprisoned my confidence. The Lord said: 'Forgive all who spoke that lie over you, then throw it away.' I prayed, then thanked him for choosing and making me, in Paul's words, an 'instrument for special purposes'. I felt much lighter and have since stopped wasting so much time.

'Godless chatter' had infected my spirit. This is why Paul wants us to 'correctly handle the word of truth', and not 'have anything to do with foolish and stupid arguments'. Words can either destroy or build up, and God's word is powerful to change lives and create beauty if we live in its truth. He is telling you that he approves of you and he made you for a noble purpose. Will you accept that as truth and let it empower you today?

Lord Jesus, thank you that you made and approve of me. In your name, I renounce every godless lie that affects or imprisons me and I choose to live in the power and love of your word of truth.

TRACY WILLIAMSON

A vision for today?

There will be terrible times in the last days. People will be lovers of themselves, lovers of money, boastful, proud, abusive, disobedient to their parents, ungrateful, unholy, without love, unforgiving, slanderous, without self-control, brutal… lovers of pleasure rather than lovers of God – having a form of godliness but denying its power. (NIV)

Are you saying 'Wow, amazing!' about Paul's vision of the last days? We expect to be awestruck by prophecies, and it *is* awesome to hear his voice, but if we think God only gives fluffy words, we are short-sighted.

Paul begins by saying, 'Mark this!' It's vital for us to take note, to expect that the state of society will be a sign of the times. We must be aware and seeking God for his purposes to be revealed. God is not trying to steal our hope for the future, but to prepare and equip us to look beyond the circumstances and partner him in his plans.

I feel shocked at how accurate Paul's description is of our present world. Every time I watch the news I see the evidence: slander, brutality, abuse, greed, control, dishonouring of parents or children, treachery…

Even we as Christians fit the bill 'having a form of godliness but denying its power'. Does that describe you? It can certainly be true of me. Once I was eating roast chicken and had the wishbone. My attention was drawn to it and a memory came of me when young, pulling the wishbone with my mum. Then God said to me: 'You pray just how you used to pull the wishbone. It was a game and even then you never expected it to work!' He added, 'I'm not a wishbone, I'm your loving heavenly Father and I love to answer your prayers!' I was stunned because it was true – I never really expected him to answer my prayers. He wanted to change me into a woman of true faith. I'm on that road now and praying is an adventure. I long to see with his eyes, and share in his unfolding plans.

What about you?

O Lord, give me eyes to see what you are doing behind the scenes. Give me faith to pray and know you will answer. I long to be your channel of love to this dark world.

TRACY WILLIAMSON

Continue in what you have learned

But as for you, continue in what you have learned and have become convinced of, because you know those from whom you learned it, and how from infancy you have known the Holy Scriptures, which are able to make you wise for salvation through faith in Christ Jesus. (NIV)

Whose teaching and lifestyle challenge you?

Following his panoramic vision of the last days, Paul urges Timothy to continue in what he has learned. Repeatedly, Paul emphasises in these letters that, while God empowers, it's Timothy's and our responsibility to live out what we've received, to let that inspiration change us.

Paul says, 'You know all about my teaching, my way of life, my purpose, faith, patience, love, endurance, persecutions, sufferings.' Paul shared his life with Timothy and now tells him to 'continue in what you have learned and have become convinced of'.

Head learning is good, but when someone's lifestyle impacts us, it creates an emotional conviction. I was taught by a well-known Christian teacher that everyone matters to God, however weak or broken. But when I visited her home and saw how she made every person feel special, it became a life-changing conviction. It is now my passion to see lonely people loved with God's love.

Another key is scripture. Paul charges Timothy to 'preach the word; be prepared in season and out of season; correct, rebuke and encourage'. It is vital to fill our hearts with God's word, even treasuring the importance of scripture that we may have learned as a child. If prayers and Bible stories were part of our childhood, their effect is still at work in us. We all need to treasure up scripture in our hearts at every opportunity.

'All scripture is God breathed,' says Paul. Are we expecting God to speak to us through his word? Today, he pinpointed a wrong attitude when I was reading 2 Samuel, and through another passage showed me how to pray. I now feel more passion to follow him than I have for years. He is so good.

Thank Jesus for the person whose faith inspires you. Ask how he wants you to change based on what you see in them.

TRACY WILLIAMSON

Awarded the crown

For I am already being poured out like a drink offering, and the time for my departure is near. I have fought the good fight, I have finished the race, I have kept the faith. Now there is in store for me the crown of righteousness. (NIV)

Paul is content with what he has accomplished in God's strength and is eagerly looking forward to his reward – the promised crown. He hands the baton of ministry to Timothy, urging him to live fully for God, to 'endure hardship, do the work of an evangelist, discharge all the duties of his ministry'.

These charges are about our attitudes as well as our actions. When life is tough, do we sink or trust that God is doing something amazing? What about our duties? I find ironing clothes very mundane, but when I do it with love it really blesses my colleague Marilyn, who is blind.

Can Timothy live life with similar passion to Paul? Can we?

The key is that God knows us and has made us to fulfil our own unique purpose. Timothy didn't need to be like Paul, but he did need to live his life fully for God. There was a crown that had his name on it, too. There's also one for you and me.

How can we be assured of that crown? What do we have to achieve? It's not to do with how many ministry successes we have! Paul's content springs from his perseverance in trusting God even when friends have deserted him or when things go wrong. He has run his race to get closer to God and demonstrate God's loveliness.

I had a dear friend who was terminally ill. She loved the Lord despite many life struggles and constantly helped others by her encouragement and prayers, yet sadly she believed she'd achieved nothing worthwhile. She did accept God's joy in her at the very end and I felt relieved she died at peace, but grieved, too, that for so long she'd been robbed of the joyful expectancy of her heavenly inheritance.

Using some paper and coloured pens, imagine yourself as a road. Draw where you started and where you are going. What kind of terrain are you passing through? Tell Jesus about it and thank him for the crown to come.

TRACY WILLIAMSON

I constantly remember you

To Timothy, my dear son… I thank God, whom I serve, as my ancestors did, with a clear conscience, as night and day I constantly remember you in my prayers. Recalling your tears, I long to see you, so that I may be filled with joy. (NIV)

To end, we'll think about Paul's closing words in 1 Timothy 6 and opening words of 2 Timothy 1. With Paul's first letter, he'd just been released from prison and was at the height of his ministry. He wanted to give Timothy godly direction. By the second letter, he was old and in prison again. He knew that his time was drawing to a close, and he wanted to bless and be blessed by Timothy.

In both letters, I've seen how certain issues like quarrelling come up repeatedly, but what stands out the most is Paul's affection towards Timothy and his desire that he lives out all that God has created him for. He was a friend and co-worker, but regarded by Paul as a son. This is a lovely picture of what Jesus feels for us. His death and resurrection mean that you now belong to him. Just as Paul writes 'my dear son', so God wants to affirm each one of us as his precious child.

Although it is vital to learn how to be a good leader, Paul teaches Timothy that it is more important to express our love for each other. Paul says, 'I constantly remember you in my prayers. Recalling your tears, I long to see you.' Paul was always praying for Timothy and, at the end of 2 Timothy 4, we see how he wants to see Timothy before he departs, saying: 'Do your best to get here.' Timothy is his spiritual son.

As I look back, I remember again that couple who took me in when I was suicidal and became spiritual parents to me, and the amazing friendship and commitment of my colleague, Marilyn. God's love through one another impacts our lives and empowers us to live for him.

Thank you, dear Father, for the wonderful gift of your friendship and love and those people in my life who love me. Please help me, like Paul with Timothy, to love, pray, affirm and believe in them by your power.

TRACY WILLIAMSON

Praying the ordinary

Jill Rattle writes:

Those of our readers who come from a church with a liturgical tradition will know that, in the church calendar, the periods between the seasons of Christmas and Easter are known as Ordinary Time. It's the ordinary times between the special times – that makes sense! The 17th-century monk, Brother Lawrence, wrote what became a Christian classic on 'praying the ordinary': *The Practice of the Presence of God*. In the things of his everyday life, he sought to be present to God because he knew in that state he would not sin.

In our daily lives, I guess most of us have more ordinary times than special times: if we didn't, the special times wouldn't be special anymore! This probably applies to your prayer life, too. It does to mine.

As we follow these notes, I'd like us to be very ordinary indeed while we look at and practise our prayer life with God. Each day for a fortnight, I have chosen something very ordinary and familiar in our lives and let it lead us into the scriptures and to prayer.

Many of us, when we're honest with ourselves and each other, admit to struggling to make prayer a priority: we struggle to make time, to still our minds, to focus on God, to intercede for others, to receive the blessing we sense is there. And then in comes the guilt, because we're sure other Christians are so much better at praying than us. Well, perhaps some of them are, but I am convinced that most Christians are like me (and you?) and struggle to make prayer our 'natural habit'.

It really isn't surprising that we often find prayer hard, because it must be one of the highest priorities of the enemy to disrupt our encounters with our Heavenly Father. All sorts of tactics will be used to keep us from prayer because 'practising the presence of God' is powerful enough to transform us and make us hugely more effective in bringing Jesus to others. Where the enemy wants to establish darkness, prayer will bring light.

So, from a personal point of view, I would like all the help I can get to make prayer my 'natural state'.

And sometimes the very ordinary can help me; I'm praying it might help you as well.

Cup

I'll lift high the cup of salvation – a toast to God! (MSG)

A cup (a mug actually) made a real difference to my prayer life. I was finding it really difficult to go into that quiet place in my house and spend time with God. One day, I realised that it was all right to have coffee with God. I could fill my cup, take it to the quiet place, sit, feel the warmth in my hands and relax in God's presence. It became a routine.

At some point today, take a cup in your hands, empty or full. What could it speak of? In the Old Testament, the image of a cup often appears symbolising the wrath of God and his judgement on the nations: Jeremiah 25, Isaiah 51 and Zechariah 12 all speak of the cup of God's wrath in this way: his judgement on the sin, the disobedience of all people.

In the garden of Gethsemane, our sinless Jesus takes that cup into his hands. It is full of all the sins, disobedience and degradation that have ever been or ever will be; your sins and mine are in that cup. No wonder he cries out to God that he might avoid drinking it. But ultimately he says, 'Yet not my will, but yours be done' (Luke 22:42, NIV). When the mob comes to arrest him and Peter cuts off the high priest's servant's ear, Jesus says, 'Put your sword away! Shall I not drink the cup the Father has given me?' (John 18:11, NIV).

And on the bitter cross, he drinks the cup of judgement to its dregs; and, gloriously, it becomes the cup of salvation for you and me and everyone before and after him, for all time.

With the psalmist, we cry, 'What can I give back to God for the blessings he's poured out on me?' Answer: my everything.

It's possible that, as today is Sunday, you will put a cup to your lips in the company of your fellow Christians. Think again what it cost Jesus to give you 'the cup of salvation'.

JILL RATTLE

Floor

It is surely true that he is my rock. He is the God who saves me. He is like a fort to me. I will always be secure. (NIRV)

Are you feeling secure and untroubled today? That's lovely. Take pleasure in that and thank God. Are you, on the other hand, feeling a bit wobbly? The situation you find yourself in seems to be shifting under your feet. You feel a bit unsteady. Or maybe it's one of those days where you have a vague sense of unease but are not quite sure what's causing it.

However you feel – good, bad or indifferent – find a seat and sit down. Plant both feet firmly on the floor. My father used to joke, 'Isn't it great that God made our legs just long enough to reach the floor?' More helpfully, someone else said, 'Let God's good earth hold you up.' Feel the solidity under your feet. You stand on the earth God created, solid and firm. He made it so it would nurture and sustain you. He made you and placed you here to be secure in his love and significant in his purposes.

Beneath your feet is the floor, beneath the floor is earth, beneath the earth is rock. Holding you up.

Read the whole of Psalm 62, if you haven't already. Look again at the extract printed above. God is my rock, the psalmist sings. Words are inadequate to describe God, so we make do with pictures and metaphors. God is rock-like: solid through and through, utterly dependable, powerful. You can 'stand' on him and be secure.

The psalmist further describes God as fortress-like. A fortress, built of stone, protecting those inside from the attacks of the enemy. If you feel under attack today or maybe tomorrow, you have a fortress to run to – God, your heavenly Father. You will not be shaken or wobble and, if you fall, call out and trust him to catch you, love you, protect you and hold you.

God, my rock. In you I trust. I will not be shaken.

JILL RATTLE

Bookshelves

From infancy you have known the Holy Scriptures, which are able to make you wise for salvation through faith in Christ Jesus. All scripture is God-breathed and is useful for teaching, rebuking, correcting and training in righteousness, so that the servant of God may be thoroughly equipped for every good work. (NIV)

As I write this, I'm living in someone else's house. Across the room are bookshelves full of her books. When I saw them, I thought: great! New books to read! But, on closer inspection, they were mostly books I'd already read and didn't fancy rereading.

But, now, in our imagination, let's replace 66 of those books with all the books of the Bible. There they are – Genesis to Revelation. They, too, are familiar books to me: I've read them since a child and I don't think I've missed any bits out, even the numbers in Numbers. But do I want to read them all again? Won't it be the same as reading those other books for the second or more time? What's the difference?

The difference is – these are alive! They are the living, breathing word of God to his people, inhabited by his Spirit, powerful enough to change all that has been and all that will be. And because I'm alive, every time I come to this amazing revelation, it has the power to change me again. Each encounter with the word of God is different from the one before. Each time, my loving Lord is speaking anew into my life, speaking his transforming, loving words over me, into me.

And yet, when I pick up my Bible or turn on my Bible app, do I always experience that tingling in my soul that tells me I am in communion with God? Honestly? No. And why is that? Probably because I don't always come with expectation; perhaps because I don't grasp just how incredible it is that God wants to speak to me through his word. Sometimes I'm like a sieve and his words seem to go through the holes. But another wise person once said to me: even a sieve needs washing!

Ask the Holy Spirit to make the word live for you, again and again – and again.

JILL RATTLE

Mirror

We don't yet see things clearly. We're squinting in a fog, peering through a mist. But it won't be long before the weather clears and the sun shines bright! We'll see it all then, see it all as clearly as God sees us, knowing him directly just as he knows us! (MSG)

Do you like looking at yourself in a mirror? I can't say I do! When I put on make-up, I use one of those two-sided mirrors. One side magnifies my face and shows up every wrinkle and blemish. I think I'd prefer the mirrors of Paul's day, which didn't give a clear reflection, hence the Bible translation 'seeing in a glass darkly'.

Of course, what I see in the mirror isn't the 'me' everyone else sees because it's the wrong way round. But even as I stare at and try to relate to my image, I'm conscious I do not fully know or understand myself. Who am I really? Why do I think like that sometimes? Why do I react that way? What would fully satisfy me? And the things I do know about myself, I don't always like. If my friends knew that about me, perhaps they wouldn't like me any more.

And it's not just me I don't understand; so much around me in the world is perplexing, confusing; I have so many questions about how things are. Why, Lord, has this happened? What sense is there in that?

For now, in God's kingdom that is 'birthed' on Earth but not yet fulfilled, I just choose to trust that our good God *does* understand, is *not* absent, *is* present to love and heal and restore, even if not in my time frame.

I am so grateful that my heavenly Father does know me completely: 'Before I formed you in the womb, I knew you' (Jeremiah 1:5, NIV). So he knows every spiritual blot and weakness in me, and yet he loves me unconditionally. That person I see in the mirror, God loves. And one day, because of what Jesus has done, I'll see him, clearly, face to face, and I'll know: this is it! I have no more questions. I am COMPLETE.

Have a look in the mirror. Say to that image, 'God loves me; I am a child of God.'

JILL RATTLE

Apron

Jesus knew that the Father had put him in complete charge of everything, that he came from God and was on his way back to God. So he got up from the supper table, set aside his robe, and put on an apron. (MSG)

Do you have an apron in the house? Do you wear it? I used to hate the idea of wearing an apron – even the word I found offensive. As for 'pinny'… Ugh!

Why? Not really sure – perhaps the connotation of subservience, low status bothered me. Oh dear – an ego problem there? I may say I wear an apron a lot these days when I bake (chef's whites and no 'pinny'!).

If there's an apron in your kitchen, take a look at it. If Jesus came to visit, and you were a bit overwhelmed and everything was a bit of a mess, would he put that apron on and start clearing up? If there was dirt on the floor, would he bend and clean it? You just know he would.

This almighty God, this creator of universes, this Lord of all, this Saviour of all mankind, has the attitude of complete humility towards us. If you doubt it, look at Philippians 2:5–11: Jesus, 'who, being in very nature God, did not consider equality with God something to be used to his own advantage; rather, he made himself nothing by taking the very nature of a servant, being made in human likeness. And being found in appearance as a man, he humbled himself by becoming obedient to death – even death on a cross!' (NIV). Jesus came down and down and down – for us.

Although 'God exalted him to the highest place' and he now sits at the right hand of the Father, he still – by his Spirit – comes to you, walks with you, clears up your mess, guides you in your choices, shares his work with you, listens to the smallest details of your life, picks you up when you fall, holds your hand in the difficult places and loves you endlessly.

There's a difference between 'serving' and 'being a servant'. You can pull in and out of serving at will. If you choose to be a servant, that's your lifelong calling. Jesus, teach me to be a servant like you.

JILL RATTLE

Teabags

Now choose life, so that you and your children may live and that you may love the Lord your God, listen to his voice, and hold fast to him. (NIV)

How simple it was once to entertain: 'How many sugars in your tea?' Done! Now it's (all in one breath): 'Tea? China India Earl Grey peppermint? Coffee? Caff decaff latte Americano cappuccino espresso…' STOP! Too much choice. We stand in the supermarket aisle, our brains bombarded by the competing brands. 'Choose me!'

So many choices to make every day, throughout our lives. Which is best? What shall I do? Who shall I choose? So many competing possibilities…

No wonder so many of us get stressed. I tease my husband that he'll go to pieces if something he purchases isn't a '*Which?* Best Buy'.

And yet, at a fundamental level, there is only one big choice to make: do we accept Jesus as Saviour God – or not? Do we choose to accept that 'living water' he offered to the woman at the well (John 4), the gift of eternal life bought for us through the cross – or not?

Once that choice is made, it affects every other life choice we make because we will want to involve him, and ask his Spirit within us to guide and help us choose rightly.

I used to worry about God's instruction in 1 Peter 1:16: 'Be holy, because I am holy.' That's impossible, I thought. How can I be holy like God? Full of light – no darkness; full of goodness – no badness; full of love – no hostility. Mostly I'm very far from holy! And then I realised that, every day, and every moment, in Jesus, I have the *potential* to be holy. At every point I can *choose* whether I am holy or unholy. Many times I'll fail and need forgiveness; but every time I ask the Spirit's help, I will be holy. And amazingly, in Jesus, God sees us already as holy.

As you look into your food cupboard today or visit the supermarket, take a moment to pray, 'Lord, help me to choose your way in all the decisions that matter.'

JILL RATTLE

Doorway (part 1)

I am the door. If anyone enters by Me, he will be saved, and will go in and out and find pasture. The thief does not come except to steal, and to kill, and to destroy. I have come that they may have life, and that they may have it more abundantly. (NKJV)

Do you ever go upstairs to get something and, by the time you get to the room, you've forgotten what you went for? Do you stand there, shaking your head in the hope that the lost item will come back to the fore? I do. Sometimes I even have to go back down stairs to rethink. Do not panic; you are not losing your memory. You have just been subject to the 'door-way effect'. Scientists have proved that passing through a door (or gate) can cause you to forget. Yes, really. Google it! It has something to do with transition from one context to another and the way the mind works (more on that tomorrow). The doorway separates one space from another and what went before can be forgotten.

Jesus says he is the door or the gate, and he uses the metaphor of the ancient sheepfold where the shepherd often lay across the threshold to keep the sheep safe in and the predators out.

There's something about 'threshold' that is really important. However short or long a walk is to a door, there is a moment when you pass from one side to the other. Individually, we have walked very different paths to come to Jesus, but there was a moment, even if we no longer recall it exactly, when what he said, recorded in John 5:24, happened for us: 'Very truly I tell you, whoever hears my word and believes him who sent me has eternal life and will not be judged but has crossed over from death to life' (NIV).

What a doorway Jesus is! And wonderfully, amazingly, graciously as our door to life, he is also the place of forgetting. He forgets: 'I will remember their sins no more!' (Hebrews 8:12, NIV). Every sin you've committed, he has forgotten!

Stand in a doorway today and thank God that he has not only forgiven your sins, but he has also forgotten them!

JILL RATTLE

Doorway (part 2)

For the present, I'm staying right here in Ephesus. A huge door of opportunity for good work has opened up here. (There is also mushrooming opposition.) (MSG)

Following on from yesterday, part of the reason we forget when passing through doorways has to do with the multi-levels our minds work on.

Let's illustrate this by imagining a woman watching three 'brickies' laying bricks. She asks each in turn what they are doing. The first responds tersely, 'I'm laying one brick on top of another.' The second smiles: 'I'm building a wall.' The third looks up with pride: 'I'm building a cathedral!'

That's how our mind works, shifting up and down between the three levels of 1) small details; 2) plans and projects; and 3) the bigger picture. No wonder we forget!

When we look at our passage for today, we can see Paul's mind running on all three levels: 1) he details for the Corinthians how to take the collection; 2) he speaks of his yet uncertain plans to visit, and the amazing opportunity (project) for evangelism that has opened up where he is, despite mounting opposition to the gospel; and 3) he makes clear in verse 10 what all this effort is about: the bigger picture is 'the work of the Lord'. Everything he is doing is for the advancement of Jesus' kingdom.

You are probably involved in church activities and projects, and, maybe, like me, you sometimes get bogged down in details and forget the bigger picture. Everything we do in Jesus' name has an eternal perspective. Even if it's small activities like taking up the collection, or picking up someone for church, they are still 'kingdom activities'; we're placing the bricks that are helping to build Jesus' kingdom. You are a kingdom builder. It's amazing that the master architect wants us to share in his great project and that he even equips us by giving us the Holy Spirit.

However, like Paul, don't be surprised if you encounter opposition in your kingdom activities.

Could you take a moment to stand in a doorway and ask Jesus what kingdom activity he wants you to undertake today? Ask him to remind you what it is all for.

JILL RATTLE

Dustbin

**And I will be merciful to them in their wrongdoings, and I will
remember their sins no more. (TLB)**

I want to take us back to this verse in Hebrews (v. 12), which I mentioned
on Saturday when we spoke of the 'doorway' being the place of forgetting, and Jesus the door, forgiving and forgetting our sins.

In a Bible study group, a friend of mine was contemplating this truth
when a picture came to mind of her bad habit. Occasionally, if she was in
a hurry, she would take a rubbish bag outside the back door and leave it
on top of an already nearly full dustbin with the intention of putting it in
properly later.

She admitted that sometimes she brought her sins to Jesus, but never
quite left them with him to dispose of, never quite accepted that they
were forgiven and out of sight for ever. She still felt guilty, remembering
what she'd done or not done.

Let's get hold firmly of the truth that God says he forgives and *forgets*
our sins. Imagine you say to Jesus: 'Lord, do you remember that horrible
mistake I made last year?'

'What mistake?' he responds.

'Lord, do you remember that unkind remark I made yesterday?'

'No, I don't.'

'Why don't you remember my sins, Lord?'

'Because, dear child, you've already repented and I've forgiven you
and wiped it from my memory. You must let it go, too.'

So many Christians are paralysed by guilt for past sins. I do think it's
right when remembering a past failure to have a moment of regret: 'I wish
that hadn't happened.' But carrying guilt that weighs us down, sinking in
our own worthlessness? No! All our guilt, all our rubbish Jesus took into
himself on the cross. He bears your guilt, not you. And he declares that,
by his grace, you are free of it. Gone!

---

*Tell Jesus of some recently confessed sin – and then thank him that he's
forgotten it.*

JILL RATTLE

Light switch

And God said, 'Let there be light!' And light appeared. (TLB)

Sometime today you will probably switch on a light (unless it's a particularly sunny October!). Maybe as you go to bed, your finger will connect with the switch and with the smallest of pressures the room will flood with light. What power you have exercised – you've turned dark to light! Something no pharaoh or Roman emperor could have done. But, of course, you know you've only played the smallest of parts in making this happen, because behind your switch is a world of technological complexity and decades of human invention that have made this wonder possible. You don't make the light.

But God does.

'The earth was a shapeless, chaotic mass,' we read, but 'the Spirit of God [was] brooding over the dark vapours.' Nothingness, it seemed, but Potential, Power, Possibility and Presence was there: God was there and he wanted physical earth-light to illustrate his eternal light. And what God says goes!

What does light do? It dispels darkness; it reveals what is there, the good and the bad; it shows the way ahead; it removes uncertainty; it makes so many things possible that the darkness prevents.

All this your electric light does when you switch it on. But what your electric light *doesn't* do is change what is there: the good remains good – your comfortable chair, your warm bed; the bad remains bad – the stain on the carpet, the damaged object.

Not so with God's light: when his light shines – into our hearts, into our situations, into our family, into our church – it changes, transforms, heals and restores.

Every morning when I wake, I pray: 'Come, Holy Spirit!', and I'm asking that the same Potential, Power, Possibility and Presence that brought light into creation will suffuse my day, fill my heart and bring glory to his name.

Lord, I open my heart to you today: where there are dark spots, please forgive me and bring your transforming light.

JILL RATTLE

Staircase

Jacob left Beersheba and set out for Haran. When he reached a certain place, he stopped for the night because the sun had set. Taking one of the stones there, he put it under his head and lay down to sleep. (NIV)

I used to prefer going downstairs to going up, but, since my knees got a bit creaky, going down is a touch painful! However, as I don't live in a bungalow, the staircase is essential from getting from one level to another. Today, my staircase offers a powerful spiritual symbol.

Jacob was in a bleak place, spiritually and physically. He was fleeing from the hatred of his brother after grossly deceiving his father, and robbing Esau of his birthright (not that Esau was entirely innocent). As night fell, Jacob found himself in a barren place with only a stone for a pillow. But then, in his dream, the place was transformed by the glory of God as a stairway appeared connecting earth to heaven, connecting Jacob to God. God repeats to him the promises he made to Abraham and lovingly promises to be with Jacob always.

When he awakes, Jacob realises: 'Surely the Lord is in this place, and I was not aware of it.' He is afraid and says, 'How awesome is this place! This is none other than the house of God; this is the gate of heaven.'

Jacob discovered that no place is so bleak, so mundane that it cannot be transformed by the glory and grace of God. Where you are now can be suffused by God's grace if you open yourself to his presence. Now is an awesome place.

What Jacob didn't know was that his dream foretold the time when Jesus would connect heaven and earth, would bring heaven to earth. Jesus makes the link with Jacob's stairway in John 1:51: 'Very truly I tell you, you will see heaven open, and the angels of God ascending and descending on the Son of Man.' Jesus is the staircase, the way to God.

As you climb the stairs today, thank Jesus that he has made a way for you to be eternally connected to God.

JILL RATTLE

My thumb

Here is a trustworthy saying that deserves full acceptance: Christ Jesus came into the world to save sinners – of whom I am the worst. (NIV)

I had the joy and privilege of being present when a brilliant Christian art therapist from Australia led a session at a women's prison that our church group visits weekly. Most prisoners there have committed serious crimes. Early in the session, the leader got us all to hold up a thumb and discover that if we lined it up with a face across the room, the thumb completely blotted it out. She said: you are not defined by the worst thing you have ever done; that thing you've done is not the whole truth about you, blotting out everything else.

Unlike those women, we probably haven't done anything in our lives that blots out all our self-worth, but sometimes something, maybe even a good thing, looms so large in our vision that it blots out our view of Jesus. It might be our job, concern for a loved one, an illness, an ambition or a responsibility. We become obsessed with it and we don't see that Jesus is there, wanting to share with us, wanting to help us get things in proportion, wanting us to see that his love is the most important thing in the world.

But if, like those women prisoners, we think we're defined by the 'bad' in us, Jesus wants us to know that's a lie. He died that our definition might be Christian – Christ in us – and we share in his holiness. Oh yes, we sin again (and again) but every time our repentance is genuine, he cleans us again.

Paul could have let himself be defined as 'murderer of Christians' and be paralysed by his past. But he accepted the free gift of Jesus' forgiving grace and went on to change the world in the Spirit's power.

Hold up your thumb and pray: Lord, help me to stop anything blotting out my vision of your love for me.

JILL RATTLE

My treasure

God's kingdom is like a treasure hidden in a field for years and then accidentally found by a trespasser. The finder is ecstatic – what a find! – and proceeds to sell everything he owns to raise money and buy that field. (MSG)

A couple of years ago, I was entranced by a television series called *The Detectorists*, starring Toby Jones as an obsessed metal detectorist hunting for elusive 'treasure' and mainly finding can ring-pulls. Eventually, his perseverance is rewarded by the thrilling find in shallow ground of a small Anglo-Saxon jewel. What he doesn't know, but what the camera shows us, is that a couple of feet below the surface is a hoard of ancient treasure! If only he had dug deeper…

It made me think that how easy it is for us Christians to settle for the little we have already discovered of God's treasures, when there is so much more to discover. We may be satisfied by seeing evidence of *one* of the fruits of the Spirit in our lives (love, joy, peace, patience, kindness, goodness, faithfulness, gentleness and self-control – see Galatians 5:22–23), when God wants to develop *all* of them in us. When did you last pray earnestly for more of that fruit?

And what about the gifts of the Holy Spirit? Yes, I know he distributes them as he chooses to his people to equip them and his church for their kingdom work. However, in 1 Corinthians 14:1, Paul writes: 'Follow the way of love and *eagerly desire gifts of the Spirit,* especially prophecy' and in verse 12, 'Since you are eager for gifts of the Spirit, try to excel in those that build up the church' (NIV).

The Spirit permits and encourages us to seek for more of God's life in us so that we can better share the good news.

As I get older, I long to 'dig deeper', to find out more of God's heart while I still have time, to know more of his grace, to experience his Spirit quickening more and more within me.

Hold in your hand one of your small 'treasures'. Hear the Lord say: I have so much more to give you, my beloved child.

JILL RATTLE

Table

Here I am! I stand at the door and knock. If anyone hears my voice and opens the door, I will come in and eat with that person, and they with me. (NIV)

I was six and in Sunday School when the teacher showed us the Holman Hunt picture of Jesus standing at the door, knocking. I was horrified to think that I had left him standing there for six whole years, and hurried to open the door! It was the beginning of sharing my life with Jesus.

But it is clear from the earlier verses in Revelation 3 that Jesus wanted to come to the people of the church of Laodicea because they were in a pitiable state of self-blindness, self-satisfaction and lethargy in their faith. Jesus found their state as unpleasant as a mouthful of something nasty – which you want to spit out.

His love for them impelled him to ask to be allowed an intimate, transforming relationship with them, and he uses the beautiful picture of being together at a table day by day to eat together. Jesus, in our hearts by his Spirit, is both guest (invited in), and host (feeding us; see Psalm 23:5).

Someone pointed out that we alone of God's creatures eat at tables. This indicates there is more to food than fuel. The table where we eat is a place of fellowship, of sharing, of enjoying each other. We give and take at a table. We laugh and talk and get to know each other.

How amazing that our sovereign God uses this picture of his desired intimacy with us. Invite me in, he says, and I will share intimately in all aspects of your daily life.

Tomorrow many of us, by his invitation, will celebrate at 'the Lord's table' his dying for us. But there is another table awaiting our presence in a glorious future: Revelation 19:9 says, 'Blessed are those who are invited to the marriage supper of the Lamb.' Yes, please!

Take a moment to sit at a table and imagine Jesus sitting across from you. Share with him what is on your heart today.

JILL RATTLE

Mountains and valleys

Christine Platt writes:

If you're fortunate enough to live within sight of a mountain or at least a decent-sized hill, I'm sure your eyes are often drawn to it. There's something about lofty peaks that inspires deeper reflection. Serene grassy valleys with munching sheep also convey images of peace and contentment.

These geographical features of Bible lands are also used as poetic symbols to illustrate more of God and his relationship with humanity. In Isaiah 54:10, we read: '"Though the mountains be shaken and the hills be removed, yet my unfailing love for you will not be shaken nor my covenant of peace be removed," says the Lord, who has compassion on you' (NIV). God's love for his people is more concrete and fixed than the most solid and immovable mountain, even ones like Everest. Mountains are also places where God had significant meetings with people: Moses and the Israelites on Mount Sinai; Jesus with Peter, James and John on the mountain of transfiguration; and 1 Kings 18—19 tells the story of God's and Elijah's almighty contest with the prophets of Baal on Mount Carmel, as well as Elijah's own private encounter with God.

Mountains and valleys can be real or metaphorical. We might describe our own experiences with God as being 'on the mountain top' when we feel God's presence in a new way, or see him at work in our lives or the lives of family and friends. Mountains can also signify difficulties in our way, like a mountain of debt. Approaching an overwhelming obstacle might feel like trying to climb Everest in beach shoes with no oxygen.

As well as providing peaceful scenes of pastoral serenity, valleys can be dark places of pain, confusion and doubt. Mountains and valleys can convey feelings of exhilaration, excitement and joy, but also the opposite – darkness, gloom, grief and desolation with which we all identify at various times of our lives.

My prayer is that as you journey through the next two weeks, reflecting on God's ways through various mountains and valleys, you will be encouraged to see more of what God wants to show you through the ups and downs of your own life. Maybe you could explore a nearby mountain, hill or valley and listen to what God wants to say to you.

Mount Carmel

So Ahab went off to eat and drink, but Elijah climbed to the top of Carmel, bent down to the ground and put his face between his knees… The servant reported, 'A cloud as small as a man's hand is rising from the sea.' (NIV)

The contrast between the prophet Elijah and King Ahab is stark. In utter rebellion against the God of Israel, Ahab introduced the worship of Baal to his people. As king, he was supposed to lead Israel in worship to the true God.

In peril of his life, Elijah confronted Ahab with his sin, and then had to live in isolation until God called him to the ultimate contest: one lonely prophet against the united forces of 450 prophets of Baal. The difference was that Elijah worshipped the God of power and the Baal prophets worshipped a nonentity. The battleground was Mount Carmel – a high point so that all could see God's clear victory and no one could deny its reality. When the people saw God hurl down fire in majestic action, they cried, 'The Lord – he is God!' (v. 39).

After this emotional high, these two men react in different ways. Ahab goes off to find food, whereas Elijah climbs to the summit of Mount Carmel to seek God and ask him to send rain to break the crippling drought in the land. Maybe he climbed to the top to get away from any distractions, but perhaps also to provide another visual picture for the spectators that God truly was the one who could answer the prayer of a human soul in quietness and without fanfare. The prophets of Baal had called on their god with loud frantic shouts and cut themselves with knives.

A small cloud appeared on the horizon and Elijah acted immediately, confident that this tiny beginning heralded a spectacular event. Elijah is an example for us in his courage, his willingness to sacrifice and his confident expectation that God would listen and answer prayer.

In your prayer life, can you see small beginnings of answers? Don't be discouraged – keep looking for them, however tiny, and trust God for their complete fulfilment.

CHRISTINE PLATT

Valley of depression

Elijah was afraid and ran for his life… he went a day's journey into the desert… and prayed that he might die. 'I have had enough, Lord. Take my life… I am the only one left, and now they are trying to kill me too.' (NIV)

From the lofty heights of spiritual victory, Elijah plunged into the depths of despair. Physical and emotional exhaustion make us vulnerable to both physical illness and mental distress. Even Elijah was not immune. How much more do we need to be alert to danger signals!

Elijah lost perspective about Jezebel's threats and she loomed larger in his thoughts and emotions than God himself. God knew what Elijah needed: he gave him food and water and sent him to sleep. Then, up on the mountain, God set Elijah's thinking straight. Elijah's ministry was not finished. God gave him a job to do and reassured him that he was not the only one left, and then gave him a friend (Elisha).

My sister recently died after a prolonged struggle. The period of her illness was exhausting in every way. After the funeral, I felt as though all the stuffing had been knocked out of me. Fortunately, I had some good friends who encouraged me to rest and not put myself under any pressure to do anything. I basically went into hibernation mode. Friends brought me meals, flowers, cards and prayed with me. Even though I knew my sister was now safe with God and at peace (hurrah!), I still needed to heal from all the trauma. The temptation was real to dwell on the sadness and pain of the more recent past rather than focus on positive memories and now her joy in being with God and our future reunion in heaven.

When you're down in the valley of sadness and grief, look up to regain God's perspective. Psalm 121:1–2 says, 'I lift up my eyes to the mountains – where does my help come from? My help comes from the Lord, the Maker of heaven and earth.'

When you are discouraged or unhappy, pray over Psalm 121 – focusing on all the promises God is giving you. Ask friends for help. Care for your physical as well as your spiritual health.

CHRISTINE PLATT

Prayer mountain

One of those days Jesus went out to a mountainside to pray, and spent the night praying to God. When morning came, he called his disciples to him and chose twelve of them, whom he also designated apostles. (NIV)

We hardly need reminding of the importance Jesus placed on prayer. Mark 1:35 recounts how he got up while it was still dark and 'went off to a solitary place, where he prayed'. There's nothing magical about climbing a mountain or walking into the wilderness to seek God, except that it ensures quietness, privacy and no distractions. Jesus had crucial decisions to make about who to choose as his disciples – the people to whom he would reveal his divine status and whom he would leave to carry on his work after his death and resurrection.

If you've ever delegated a job to anyone, you'll know it sometimes isn't easy who to choose. Do they have the skills? Are they enthusiastic and teachable? Will they be faithful in the long term? Many were following Jesus, eager to hear his teaching and to witness his miracles, but out of all these, who to choose as his inner circle?

There's no doubt that prayer played a vital part in Jesus' decision-making – which is an important example for us to follow. He also waited all night for clarity. Sometimes we are forced into quick decisions, but usually there is time to wait. If it's a yes/no decision, I sometimes live for a day or two with 'Yes' in my mind. I've found this really helps. Other factors pop into my thoughts that I hadn't considered, or I get a greater sense of peace or lack of peace than before. Then I'll live for a day or two with 'No' as the answer, and see what transpires. In any event, waiting is usually a good move. 'Wait for the Lord; be strong and take heart and wait for the Lord,' says Psalm 27:14.

'Trust God from the bottom of your heart; don't try to figure out everything on your own. Listen for God's voice in everything you do, everywhere you go; he's the one who will keep you on track' (Proverbs 3:5–6, MSG).

CHRISTINE PLATT

Valley of trouble

Achan replied, 'It is true! I have sinned against the Lord… This is what I have done: when I saw in the plunder a beautiful robe… silver… [and] gold… I coveted them and took them. They are hidden in the ground inside my tent.' (NIV)

'I saw, I coveted, I took, I hid.' This was the progression of Achan's sin. He may well have started well and fought bravely, but then got sidetracked and compromised. The consequences of his sin were vastly greater than he ever imagined. He may have thought, 'These are just a few things to steal; no one will know.'

It is easy for us to rationalise sin or seek to minimise it. What seems insignificant in our eyes – like ignoring road safety rules – may have dire outcomes. We hear tragic stories of people texting while driving and ending up smashed to smithereens, bringing grief and pain to their families and friends as well as cutting short their own and even other people's lives. Rules and instructions are given for our safety even though they may seem irksome at times.

Also, let's think about relationships. People don't generally suddenly decide to be unfaithful. Things start small and, unless checked, can escalate exponentially. We go from seeing, to coveting, to taking and then trying to hide it.

So, what could Achan have done? He could have reminded himself of the instructions: 'Keep away from the devoted things… All the silver and gold… are sacred to the Lord and must go into his treasury' (Joshua 6:18–19). Then he could have turned his eyes away. Being tempted is our human experience because we have an enemy who seeks to trip us up at every turn. The sin comes when we allow the temptation to linger and then act on it. We end up in the valley of trouble. But if we turn to God, he promises to send help.

'No test or temptation that comes your way is beyond the course of what others have had to face… God will never let you down… He'll always be there to help you come through it' (1 Corinthians 10:13, MSG).

CHRISTINE PLATT

Mount Sinai

And God spoke all these words: 'I am the Lord your God, who brought you out of Egypt, out of the land of slavery. You shall have no other gods before me.' (NIV)

At Mount Sinai, God gave the Israelites – and, by extension, all of us – his ten rules for living. Unfortunately, ever since God gave them, humanity has consistently failed to obey them. Yet all of the world's hideous problems would be solved by simply following these ten rules. People wouldn't get burned out if we all took one day off a week to rest. World hunger and poverty would disappear because we wouldn't be greedy and there would therefore be enough for everyone.

There would be no refugees or internally displaced people because we wouldn't steal or murder. Every home would be secure and a haven for its members; there would be no adultery; parents would be honoured.

Why do we ignore these sensible and life-giving rules? I think the foundation stone is the first one: 'You shall have no other gods before me.' It's sad to say, but, for most of us, we put ourselves on the throne at least some of the time. If and when God is number one in our lives, the other rules follow on automatically.

If our first priority is to love and obey God, then we will naturally treat other people well and be content with what God gives us. We would also be kind to ourselves and take time to rest and be refreshed and not fall into the 'I've got to be a busy Christian' trap. I've done more than my fair share of that. Who do we think we are? Do we know better than God how to live life on this planet that he has so generously provided for us? Obviously we can't change the world singlehandedly, but we can all eject ourselves from the throne and put God in his rightful place.

Father God, I want to learn to love you with all my heart, my soul and my mind and also to love my neighbour as myself. Help me to recognise when I am pleasing myself and not you.

CHRISTINE PLATT

Valley of praise (Berakah)

As they began to sing and praise, the Lord set ambushes against the men… who were invading Judah, and they were defeated… They [King Jehoshaphat and the army of Judah] assembled in the Valley of Berakah, where they praised the Lord. (NIV)

Often when I listen to the news, I despair of the state of our world. We seem to make progress on one front – for example, there are fewer people living in absolute poverty now than there were a decade ago – but then another conflict or disaster happens somewhere else and we witness the inevitable tide of human suffering yet again. The problems seem immense and never-ending.

Jehoshaphat, king of Judah, may well have looked in panic at the vast army coming against him and been tempted to despair. But he didn't collapse into a grovelling heap and capitulate. He took decisive action. He summoned his people together and they all prayed for God's intervention. God answered through Jahaziel and promised deliverance. The king and the people trusted God for a miracle and worshipped him. The circumstances hadn't changed. The vast army was still on its way, but now they had God's promise. As they went out to fight, they began to sing and praise – unusual tactics for an army! God confused the enemy and they ended up destroying each other.

This is a lesson for all of us. Our enemy wants to discourage us and cause us to believe that nothing will ever improve. But we need to face each day with the conviction that God has not abandoned our planet. He is at work. Good things are happening. Sadly, the media doesn't always consider positive stories to be newsworthy. So, instead of being disheartened, feeling the weight of the world's pain on my shoulders, I need to sing, to worship and praise God for his abounding greatness and love and remember that nothing is too hard for him (Jeremiah 32:27).

Look out for some good news stories this week and remember to give thanks to God for his intervention. Start each day focusing on God's promises and power. We are on the winning side!

CHRISTINE PLATT

Temptation mountain

The Devil took him on the peak of a huge mountain… pointing out all the earth's kingdoms… He said, 'They're yours… just go down on your knees and worship me.' Jesus' refusal was curt… 'Worship the Lord your God, and only him. Serve him with absolute single-heartedness.' (MSG)

Do you sometimes take shortcuts either on a trip or when doing a job? I confess I do. Sometimes it works out okay, but more often the journey or the task takes longer and I end up wasting time, money and energy.

Satan offered Jesus a shortcut – a quick solution to let the world know who he was – when he promised to make Jesus a political leader. Whether Satan had the power to do that is debatable. He could have just been living up to his name – the father of lies (John 8:44). Jesus was not fooled. His main purpose was to save the world from sin, and political power was not the answer. He knew the only way to fulfil God's plan for his life was to serve him with absolute single-heartedness, whatever the cost. Nothing worthwhile is accomplished with a quick fix.

Neither are there shortcuts to developing a close relationship with God. A hasty prayer here and there or a brief glance at a Bible verse won't do the trick. Absolute single-heartedness means making time for God on a daily basis – just as you are doing now while reading these notes. I hope you also have time to do the full Bible reading.

Bible reading and prayer are part of the answer. Jesus knew the scriptures, but even he had to put them into practice, which meant saying a definite NO to Satan and a big YES to God. God isn't interested in enlarging our brains with knowledge. He wants to transform our lives to be more like Jesus. As we think deeply about God's word, he will show us ways to implement his values in our daily lives.

Father God, open my eyes and my mind as I read your word, and help me to put into practice whatever you show me. Give me understanding so that I obey you and am not sidetracked by the enemy.

CHRISTINE PLATT

Elah Valley

David said to the Philistine, 'You come against me with sword and spear... but I come against you in the name of the Lord Almighty, the God of the armies of Israel, whom you have defied. This day... the whole world will know that there is a God in Israel.' (NIV)

A few years ago, I had the great privilege of visiting Israel. One of the sites we went to was the Elah Valley, where this famous battle took place. I picked up a stone from the brook and brought it home. I'm looking at it now as I write these notes. It's such a plain, ordinary little thing with no power of its own. Yet in David's – and ultimately God's – hands, an insignificant stone delivered the killer blow. I can imagine an angel being dispatched to make sure the stone hit exactly the right spot – the only point of vulnerability in Goliath's armour!

How did David have such courage when all the soldiers, and King Saul himself, quailed before this colossal adversary? I think from David's explanation to Saul (vv. 34–37), he had had many opportunities to trust God against formidable opponents – lions and bears – while he just did his normal day job. During those years of caring for sheep in obscurity, God had trained his man. David had learned that God could be relied upon. So when the big public battle came, David was ready to step up.

This perspective ennobles our daily responsibilities. Jesus said, 'Whoever can be trusted with very little can also be trusted with much' (Luke 16:10). David could have felt that looking after sheep was a very menial job, but he did it conscientiously. God can use whatever you are doing right now to prepare you for greater opportunities in the future. The only prerequisite is to be faithful and do your best, however small or large the task.

This doesn't mean that we should take on every Goliath that comes our way. David was sure God was leading him to oppose this Goliath and therefore he could be confident of victory.

Lord, thank you for the opportunities you give me today to be faithful and work diligently. Please help me to recognise – and be courageous – when you want me to step up.

CHRISTINE PLATT

Transfiguration mountain

[Jesus] climbed the mountain to pray, taking Peter, John and James along… The appearance of his face changed and his clothes became blinding white. At once two men were there talking with him. They turned out to be Moses and Elijah – and what a glorious appearance they made! (MSG)

The word 'awesome' is used in many contexts – even to describe ice cream! But this event was truly awesome. Peter, James and John could scarcely believe their eyes. They were speechless. They'd gone up a mountain for a prayer time and come back changed men. Yes, Jesus was transformed into his shining glory, but the disciples were also transformed in their understanding of who Jesus really was.

Maybe they'd got used to seeing miracles, but this was on another scale: Jesus in radiant splendour and God enveloping them in a 'light-radiant cloud' and declaring, 'This is my Son, the Chosen! Listen to him.'

What makes you awestruck and speechless? For me, it's often nature – crimson sunsets or the intricacy, beauty and fragrance of roses. I'm often also awestruck by people's kindness and their willingness to sacrifice their own comfort, and even their own lives, for others. I see God in that.

Maybe we all need a daily dose of 'awestruckness' to lift our eyes above the mundane. Our God gives us daily reminders of his awesomeness. Often we rush by without noticing and hasten on to the next task/activity, even if only to check who has posted a message on Facebook! It's not that we are going to sit and worship a rose, but that we recognise the creative beauty of God and his generosity in giving us evidence of his character.

It's unlikely that we will see Jesus in his splendour in this life, but maybe stopping for a moment to savour transcendent moments would bring balance to hassled lives. What might make you stop and think 'Wow'? Turn your thoughts to God and thank him for it.

Look out for 'wow' moments today. Take time, even a few extra seconds, to linger and enjoy whatever experiences God brings across your path.

CHRISTINE PLATT

Valley of dry bones

The Lord… brought me out by the Spirit of the Lord and set me in the middle of a valley; it was full of bones… He asked me, 'Son of man, can these bones live?' I said, 'Sovereign Lord, you alone know.' (NIV)

The people of Israel were in a bleak situation. Jerusalem had been conquered and destroyed by Cyrus the Persian and the citizens were in exile. They lamented, 'Our bones are dried up and our hope is gone' (v. 11). They saw no prospect of returning to their land and living in freedom and peace. They were hopeless and helpless. Those in refugee camps today must feel equally lost and abandoned, with only a meagre hope for a better life. However, hope is as vital to life as food and drink. Fyodor Dostoevsky wrote: 'To live without hope is to cease to live.'

Into this pit of despair, Ezekiel brings a message of hope to the exiles. He correctly answers God's question 'Can these bones live?' with 'O Sovereign Lord, you alone know.' God was the only one who could get them out of this mess. He alone could engineer world events to bring them back to the land of Israel, which he did. This message must have been like a cool drink on a scorching day to those suffering in exile. Yet, maybe some were so discouraged they couldn't rouse themselves to believe.

I can't fully identify with how desperate they may have felt, but perhaps you can. Maybe your hope has been all but extinguished by pressure, sadness and pain. God has the same message for you as he had for his beleaguered people. In Ezekiel's vision, the dry bones did come together, breath entered them, they came to life and they stood up on their feet – a vast army. He is the God of hope. With him in the equation, there is always a reason for hope. Things may not improve today or tomorrow but, in his time, he will fulfil his promise.

Memorise this verse – 'May the God of hope fill you with all joy and peace as you trust in him, so that you may overflow with hope by the power of the Holy Spirit' (Romans 15:13).

CHRISTINE PLATT

Mount Moriah

God said [to Abraham], 'Take your son, your only son, whom you
love – Isaac – and go to the region of Moriah. Sacrifice him there'…
So Abraham called that place, The Lord Will Provide. (NIV)

Mount Moriah is a hugely significant biblical site. It is in the old city of
Jerusalem and one of the most hotly fought-over areas of real estate on
earth. It is deeply sacred to Jews, Christians and Muslims.

We first encounter Mount Moriah in Abraham's time, when it was just
a mountain which was about to witness an almost unimaginable act of
devotion. God had no intention that Isaac would be harmed. He was
deepening Abraham's faith and obedience which would make him worthy
to be called the 'Father of Faith': 'through your offspring all nations on
earth will be blessed, because you have obeyed me' (v. 18). Through that
extraordinary act of courage and sacrifice, you and I and all people have
been blessed by God.

God still blesses faith and obedience today, through our willingness to
put him first. He invites us to give up some of our money, time, energy,
desires and goals in order that others can receive a blessing. For years,
I questioned why God didn't bring along some godly dishy man for me to
marry and create a family with. Eventually I surrendered and said: 'If I can
serve you best as a single person, okay.' Not exactly joyful surrender, but
surrender nonetheless! But it's not a once-and-for-all-time experience.
Different stages of life bring the need for fresh levels of surrender.

Obviously God wants us to give up bad things which harm us and others, but also sometimes he puts his finger on good and legitimate things
and asks us to trust him to be the Lord who provides – perhaps not in the
way hoped for.

---

*Is God inviting you to a Mount Moriah moment? Is there an area of sacrifice
and surrender that he wants you to trust him for? Our vision is so limited,
whereas God sees the big picture. Will you trust him?*

CHRISTINE PLATT

Valley of Megiddo

[Necho said] 'It is not you I am attacking… so stop opposing God, who is with me, or he will destroy you.' [Josiah] would not listen to what Necho had said at God's command but went to fight him on the plain of Megiddo. Archers shot King Josiah. (NIV)

The Megiddo Valley has had a tumultuous history. It has been the site of numerous battles over the centuries. It's on a strategic trade route and everybody wanted it. It's a vast flat area, also known as Jezreel Valley, with a town called Megiddo where 26 layers of civilisation have been excavated.

Josiah was one of the better kings of Israel. He had instituted a wholesale reform of the temple worship and got rid of all the false idols from the land – good man! But after such a faithful and courageous life of service to God, he seems to have had a brain fade. He marched out with his army to fight against Necho, king of Egypt. Necho was not attacking him and God warned Josiah against going into battle. But Josiah insisted, persisted with his own plans and was killed – a tragic and untimely end.

Did he think, 'Ah well, I've done a lot for God, now I can do what I want', or perhaps, 'I know better than God what needs to be done around here'? An enthusiastic beginning does not guarantee a positive end. 1 Corinthians 10:12 alerts us: 'So, if you think you are standing firm, be careful that you don't fall!' Even the best of us can make the mistake of trusting ourselves rather than remaining in moment-by-moment dependence upon God.

However we serve, whether with our youthful energy or with the wisdom of our mature years, we still need to be wholehearted right to the end ('Whatever you do, work at it with all your heart', Colossians 3:23), seeking God's will and not our own ('Yet not what I will, but what you will', Mark 14:36).

Thank you, Lord, that you accept my love and service at whatever stage of life I am, however capable or incapacitated I might be. Help me to finish my earthly pilgrimage well and make every day count for you.

CHRISTINE PLATT

Mount of Olives

As he approached Jerusalem and saw the city, he wept over it and said, 'If you, even you, had only known on this day what would bring you peace… You did not recognise the time of God's coming to you.' (NIV)

The Mount of Olives was a significant place in Jesus' life. He taught his disciples there (Matthew 24—25). He prayed in the Garden of Gethsemane, which is at the foot of the mountain. He made his triumphal entry down its slopes into Jerusalem on a donkey on Palm Sunday. The present-day view from the Mount of Olives over to Jerusalem is spectacular and probably one of the most photographed sights on earth. But when Jesus looked at the city, he wept. Beyond its architectural beauty, he saw its spiritual state and, consequently, its tragic future. His prophecy of destruction (vv. 43–44) was fulfilled when the Romans destroyed the city in AD70. Today, it continues to be the focus of antagonism.

Why did Jesus weep? Because the Jewish people did not recognise the time of God's coming to them. They were expecting a different type of messiah. They had preconceived ideas about what he would be like, so they rejected the one God provided.

Do you sometimes find that your image of who God is and what he is like doesn't stack up with reality? Mystery swirls around God and, however much we want to put him in a box, he will not fit in there. We look at our world and it seems out of control with evil triumphing on every side. We see loved ones suffering ghastly diseases and addictions and, in spite of our fervent prayers, they are not always healed.

I wonder if this should challenge us to expand our view of God and acknowledge that he sees the bigger picture. Could it be that God comes to us in our questionings and pain with fresh revelation of himself? We don't understand, but he does – and will, in the end, make everything right.

Father God, help me not to miss what you're trying to show me when I face pain or confusion. Help me not to be too rigid or closed in my thinking, but to be open to new insights.

CHRISTINE PLATT

Sermon on the mount

You're here to be salt-seasoning that brings out the God-flavours of this earth. If you lose your saltiness, how will people taste godliness? You've lost your usefulness... You're here to be light, bringing out the God-colours in the world. God is not a secret to be kept. (MSG)

Are you on a low-salt diet for your heart health? I am. It takes a bit of getting used to. Salt makes food so tasty, as all the potato chip manufacturers know! We crave that flavour. In a similar way, humanity craves love, peace, joy and hope – all of which are found in God. They are his flavours. But most people don't realise that a friendship with God is the answer to their craving. They search in many other directions – wealth, relationships, buying new stuff, entertainment, and so on.

In his sermon on the mount, Jesus says his followers are to be 'salt-seasoning that brings out the God-flavours of this earth' and 'light, bringing out God-colours in the world'. It should be obvious that God is in partnership with us.

Paradoxically, when we're being kind, loving and helpful, it's easy for people to praise us – 'You're such a good person' – rather than recognise that God is the source. I've discovered I need to find short phrases that don't sound too pious to deflect the praise onto the worthy recipient, namely Jesus. I'm still working on this, but a simple phrase like 'Well, actually God helps me' may be all that's needed for them to see that it's not my innate goodness that's at work – far from it! We're here to bring out God's colours and God's flavours, so that people see him and not us.

And how can we become more salty and shine more brightly? Let's ask Jesus to work in us using his Spirit to produce godly qualities and make us more like him. Only in that way will others be drawn to the Saviour and will their craving be satisfied.

Lord Jesus, make me more loving, joyful, peaceful, patient, kind, good, gentle, faithful and self-controlled, so I can more truly reflect you to the world around me (Galatians 5:22–23).

CHRISTINE PLATT

Daniel

Katy Jack writes:

I am reviewing these notes on holiday. We are staying in a great campsite in the beautiful Ardéche region of France. As I write, the sun is shining, I am by the pool and the boys are all playing Boggle with their dad – perfect! The Jack family are strangers in a foreign land, but we are in no way exiles. We chose to go on holiday, we drove ourselves (a long way!) to a campsite we chose, and we know that on Wednesday evening we will be on the ferry back home to Poole.

Not so the exiles in the book of Daniel.

The people of Israel, the people of God, have been increasingly led astray by the nations around them. They have worshipped foreign gods, adopted their neighbours' ways and habits, and have tacked on the Lord Almighty, who made and saved them, as an optional extra – like a superstitious lucky charm.

After centuries of their disobedience, God finally brings judgement on his people – by now split into two kingdoms. The northern kingdom has already been invaded and taken into exile by Assyria. In 625BC, the Babylonian empire overtakes Assyria as the main superpower, and the king of Babylon, Nebuchadnezzar, wastes no time in invading the southern kingdom of Judah.

God's people find themselves as strangers in a foreign land – exiles far from their physical and spiritual land. Was God really in control? Was he still faithful to his promises? Did he still care?

And the answer Daniel gives us is a resounding 'Yes!'

I have loved studying Daniel. The first six chapters are accounts of Daniel and his friends in the court of Babylon. The last four chapters are visions of the future – giving us a glimpse into the court of heaven. It's a book full of encouragement, hope and calls to stand firm, persevere and be patient as we wait for God's glorious kingdom to come.

We won't have time to finish the whole book in our fortnight together, but my prayer is that the first eight chapters of this great book will be a huge encouragement to us as Christian women as we live as exiles in this 21st-century world, far from, but looking forward to, our spiritual home of heaven.

Get stuck in – God is in control!

In the third year of the reign of Jehoiakim king of Judah, Nebuchadnezzar king of Babylon came to Jerusalem and besieged it. And the Lord delivered Jehoiakim king of Judah into his hand. (NIV)

The unimaginable has happened. King Nebuchadnezzar has come to Jerusalem and besieged it. He even dared to raid the holy temple of God and take sacred articles as trinkets to decorate the temple of his Babylonian god. To add insult to injury, he takes the crème de la crème of Jerusalem society as captives back to Babylon to absorb into his civil service. Disaster! Humiliation! Where is God in all this? Verse 2 gives us the surprise answer: God was right there delivering his people over to the king of Babylon just as, in love, he warned that he would.

Daniel and his friends, probably not more than 14 years of age, find themselves in a foreign land and far from the external structures and support of their family and religion: a small minority group, placed in an alien and hostile environment. How will they fare? Will they be swallowed up and become just like all the other Babylonians? Will they retreat into a safe holy huddle and hope for the best? No! Just as God told the later exiles through the prophet Jeremiah (29:1–7), Daniel and his friends get stuck in. They accept their new job offer, throw themselves into the education system and they even accept their new Babylonian names.

God doesn't call us to live in a holy huddle, insulated from the world 'out there'. He calls us to be a blessing to the world in which he has placed us. Get to know your neighbours, make friends at the school gate, welcome people into your home, be an excellent employee, serve at the local sports club, sing in the local choir. God is in control of where he puts his people. You live where you live because God has put you there – get stuck in!

Dear Lord, thank you for the opportunity to live in your world today. Help me to get stuck in and make a difference today.

KATY JACK

Drawing a line

But Daniel resolved not to defile himself with the royal food and wine, and he asked the chief official for permission not to defile himself in this way. (NIV)

Daniel and his friends got stuck in, but they also drew a line. They were not prepared to eat the food and the wine from the royal table. The Jewish Torah contains strict food laws and they were not prepared to disobey God by eating non-kosher food sacrificed to idols. Politely, but resolutely, Daniel drew the line and asked for permission not to defile himself in this way. He absolutely trusted God for the outcome.

I expect some people mocked and ridiculed these young men. 'What's your problem? Where's the harm in a little food and wine? You don't need to take your religion that seriously! Relax a little – you are in Babylon now.'

Where do you need to draw the line in your life in order to live wholeheartedly for God in a way that honours and brings glory to him? It might be in relation to how much you drink in social situations, being careful of the relationships you allow to develop, being aware of the impact of certain films or internet sites on your godliness, noting where social media cultivates a spirit of discontent.

It may be that others think you are a bit extreme or full-on for drawing such a line. You may be mocked or ridiculed. We should be prepared for that reaction from the world. But allow the wonderful vindication of these four Hebrew boys to encourage you. Not only does God help them through the ten-day test that the official sets for their request, but he also blesses them with wonderful knowledge and understanding. So much so that when the king meets the four God-honouring, vegetarian, watersipping lads, he is blown away by their wisdom and understanding. They stand head and shoulders above all the other advisers in his kingdom.

Spend some time thinking and praying about where you might need to draw the line in your life, trusting that God will honour your desire to live wholeheartedly for him.

KATY JACK

Horizon filler

'Praise be to the name of God for ever and ever; wisdom and power are his. He changes times and seasons; he deposes kings and raises up others. He gives wisdom to the wise and knowledge to the discerning.' (NIV)

Nebuchadnezzar is the most powerful man in the world. His empire stretches across much of the known world; his military might seems unstoppable. But today we find him troubled, unable to sleep, paranoid and desperate. None of his apparently wise men can help him and tell him the content and meaning of the dream that haunts him. They cry out to their own gods, but only God has the answer. The king is so angry that no one can help him that he issues a decree for all the wise men to be executed.

When Daniel hears of the king's decree and his own impending death, he doesn't panic. He is courteous and calm. He asks for time and goes straight to his friends to ask them to join him in prayer, pleading with God for mercy and a revelation of the king's dream.

Marvel at how his trust in God and the power of prayer are vindicated. That very night, the dream is revealed to Daniel and he bursts out with praise for his great God.

Even though he is facing a very angry, irrational and powerful king, Daniel doesn't doubt his God. He knows that God controls everything and that true wisdom comes only from God. He has such a big view of God that God fills his horizons, keeping in perspective anything or anyone else who could intimidate or threaten him.

What threatens to dominate your horizon today? A person, an illness, financial worries, difficulties in relationships or at work? Does the threat seem overwhelming? Like Daniel, why not go to praying, godly friends and ask them to plead with you for mercy from the God of heaven? Echo Daniel's prayer of praise and allow God to fill your horizon.

Spend some time contemplating Daniel's prayer in verses 20–23 and ask the awesome God who Daniel describes to fill your horizons today.

KATY JACK

The revealer of mysteries

Surely your God is the God of gods and the Lord of kings and a revealer of mysteries, for you were able to reveal this mystery. (NIV)

The Assyrians, Babylonians, Medes, Persians, Greeks, Romans. What do they all have in common? They were all once vast and powerful empires whose remnants are now on display for tourists in the British Museum. God knew that would be the case and he revealed it to the great king of Babylon in the dream which Daniel interpreted.

There is much we could look at from this passage, but today we are going to focus on two points.

Firstly, the wonder of Jesus' kingdom. His is the rock that breaks all the other kingdoms. His is the kingdom which will never be destroyed and will endure forever. Jesus retaught these truths 600 years after Daniel, when he walked on this earth and spoke in parables explaining the nature of the kingdom of heaven. King Jesus' kingdom may have a small and unimpressive start, like a little bit of yeast or a small mustard seed, but its expansion is wonderful and unstoppable, and it will outlast and supersede all worldly kingdoms and empires.

Secondly, the wonder of God's revelation. Nebuchadnezzar was bowled over by what he glimpsed of Daniel's God through this interpretation. The God of the Bible is not a secretive, covert god who keeps his cards close to his chest. He wants to reveal himself and his will to his creation. Ultimately, we see this as he delights to reveal the mystery of his will – to bring all things in heaven and earth under the perfect rule of King Jesus.

Whose kingdom are you living in? An earthly kingdom which will one day pass away and be forgotten? Or Christ's eternal kingdom where our citizenship starts the moment we put our trust in him and will continue for our whole lifetime, through death and into eternity?

Read Ephesians 1:3–10 and meditate on the wonder of God's revealed will to us in the Bible.

KATY JACK

Protection through the furnace

'If we are thrown into the blazing furnace, the God we serve is able to save us from it… But even if he does not, we want you to know, Your Majesty, that we will not serve your gods or worship the image of gold you have set up.' (NIV)

When I read accounts of brothers and sisters around the world who are treated terribly by the authorities simply because they are Christians, I am blown away by their courage. Would I be able to cope if ever God allowed me to suffer in that way?

In today's chapter, Nebuchadnezzar invents a new religion. He wants the Babylonian Empire to be a strong, united society. He thinks that enforcing a common religion on everyone will be a great unifier. There's a golden thing to bow down to, a worship band and a call to worship. The threat of a fiery furnace acts as a not-so-subtle incentive to conformity.

Similarly, in some countries today, Christians face the threat of death simply for being Christian. While Christians in many other countries don't face that level of threat, they and we must increasingly contend with laws which ostensibly aim to create a 'cohesive' and 'united' society but which produce a society conforming out of pressure or fear. Failure to conform may result in threats of loss of employment or business and the imposition of fines or imprisonment. Some newly imposed laws raise difficult decisions for Christians today.

Shadrach, Meshach and Abednego give us a great lesson in what we should do when faced with laws which seem to fly in the face of worshipping God. They are bold and brave. They are utterly faithful to God and absolutely clear that they will not worship anything other than him.

God doesn't protect them from the fiery furnace. But when they are in the furnace, he draws right alongside them and protects them through the furnace. Many Christians can testify that, as they went through their own furnace experience, they knew God was closely with them, giving grace sufficient for all that they faced.

Dear Lord, please help me to live all-out for you today, even if it lands me in a metaphorical furnace. Help me to trust that you, my loving protector God, will be right there with me as I face the heat.

KATY JACK

Speaking the truth in love

Therefore, Your Majesty, be pleased to accept my advice: renounce your sins by doing what is right, and your wickedness by being kind to the oppressed. It may be that then your prosperity will continue. (NIV)

Yet again, Nebuchadnezzar is haunted by a worrying dream and his Babylonian wise men are unable to help him. Finally (he's a slow learner), he asks Daniel to interpret the dream for him. You can imagine the awkward pause after Nebuchadnezzar has described the disturbing dream. Daniel knows exactly what it means and it's not exactly going to be a picnic in the park for the king.

The temptation might have been to shy away from a clear answer, but Daniel does the loving thing – he warns Nebuchadnezzar of the impending judgement. Unless Nebuchadnezzar changes his ways, he is going to suffer a terrible mental breakdown which will last until he acknowledges that only God is sovereign.

Despite this clear warning to repent, from someone whom Nebuchadnezzar deeply respects, the king ignores the warning. A whole year passes and, as he stands on the roof of his palace, he proudly gives himself all the credit for the empire he has built for his glory. Pride comes before a fall, and Nebuchadnezzar's fall is great. He becomes mad and is driven away from people to live like a wild animal. The great king Nebuchadnezzar eats grass like a cow.

God graciously warns all people of the need to repent and acknowledge him as God. He is patient and doesn't want any to perish. But a day will come when his judgement will be enacted. Speaking the truth in love can be very hard. Pray for courage to be like Daniel and to share the truth of God's judgement, forgiveness and love with others. As tomorrow's reading shows, the results could be utterly thrilling!

Sovereign God, I praise you as the Most High God and sovereign over all people. Please help me to share this truth in love with family and friends.

KATY JACK

Coming to faith

Now I, Nebuchadnezzar, praise and exalt and glorify the King of heaven, because everything he does is right and all his ways are just. And those who walk in pride he is able to humble. (NIV)

I love hearing how people have become Christians, which is perhaps why I find today's verses such a source of joy. Each spiritual journey back to God is unique, a miracle of people passing from death to life. Testimonies are such a clear example of God's grace to sinners like you and me.

Imagine picking up the newspaper, watching the breakfast news or scrolling through your Twitter feed and every headline is the same. The story that has gone viral is that the most powerful person in the world has come to faith and wants the world to know!

Nebuchadnezzar has become a believer! It's his great pleasure to tell everyone about the miraculous signs and wonders that God has performed in his life.

Pause here to remember yesterday's study. Nebuchadnezzar has not had an easy few years; God hasn't performed health and wealth miracles in his life. Instead, God has humbled Nebuchadnezzar through a terrible mental illness. But he can see now, looking back, that God, in his sovereign wisdom, used the trial to bring him to faith.

Nebuchadnezzar's conversion was slow and messy. He took steps towards grasping something about Daniel's God and then seemed to leap backwards making crazy anti-God laws. But over the years, he moved forward. He changed from a temple-pillaging, idol-worshipping, proud and arrogant king to a humble leader, singing God's praises.

Have you been praying for a neighbour or family member for years? Have you seen them taking steps towards Jesus and then leaping backwards? Do you despair that they may never come to Christ? Let Daniel's faithful and steadfast witness to King Nebuchadnezzar be an encouragement to you to keep getting stuck in, holding the line, speaking the truth and worshipping the one true God.

Spurred on by the conversion of King Nebuchadnezzar, spend some time praying for family and friends who you long to come to Christ.

KATY JACK

No spiritual grandchildren

But you, Belshazzar, his son, have not humbled yourself, though you knew all this. Instead, you have set yourself up against the Lord of heaven… You did not honour the God who holds in his hand your life and all your ways. (NIV)

The humbling of King Nebuchadnezzar had a happy ending. The humbling of Nebuchadnezzar's son, King Belshazzar, is a very different story.

We are introduced to the new king as he toasts gods that are not gods at all, and gets drunk using goblets from the Lord God's temple in Jerusalem. It's a tragic picture. Belshazzar would have heard from his own father all about the true God of heaven, but he turns his back on the God his father worshipped, casts his most godly and wise adviser into the political wilderness and focuses on living it up, throwing an enormous banquet.

The sad thing about this story is that, although Daniel calmly and clearly interprets the terrifying writing on the wall, Belshazzar does not respond to the warning. Daniel exposes his pride, his rejection of God and the impending disaster. But Belshazzar doesn't repent. Instead, he seems to try to deflect attention from the embarrassing prophecy by lavishing robes, gold and positions of authority on Daniel.

Wasn't he listening?! Now was not the time to start rejigging the civil service! Now was the time to bow in humility before the God who held his life and all his ways in his hands.

The Israelites may be in exile, but God is still in control. Just as the writing on the wall predicted, that very night Belshazzar is killed, the great Babylonian empire comes to a crashing halt and a new superpower enters the world stage.

Belshazzar was not immune from God's judgement because his dad was a believer. If we have had the privilege of being brought up in a Christian home or of having our own children, let's remember that our salvation depends not on our family connections but on God's grace alone.

Pray for your children, grandchildren, godchildren or children in your church family – that they realise their need to personally repent and put their trust in Jesus.

KATY JACK

Expect opposition

They could find no corruption in him, because he was trustworthy and neither corrupt or negligent. Finally these men said, 'We will never find any basis for charges against this man Daniel unless it has something to do with the law of his God.' (NIV)

Kingdoms come and kingdoms go. Daniel, God's man in Babylon, has out-lasted the two Babylonian kings and is now serving in the civil service of King Darius the Mede.

How is Daniel faring? He has been living in Babylon for decades. Has he lost his love for the Lord? Has his faith been battered and shipwrecked in the face of constant opposition? Has he 'calmed down' after his youthful 'religious phase'?

Wonderfully, no! These first few verses of chapter 6 reveal Daniel faithfully serving God by being a godly and excellent employee. The times around him are constantly changing, but Daniel is constantly constant. You would think that would be a really great thing, that his colleagues would enjoy working with such an honest, hard working man full of integrity. But they don't.

These verses give us a really helpful reality check. We clearly see that living faithfully for God will lead to some people hating us. See how the satraps and the administrators are jealous of Daniel's position in Darius' court. They determine to catch him out, to expose him publicly. But they can't find any dirt to dish. The only 'weak spot' they can find is his faith.

I am a terrible people-pleaser. I don't like conflict and I like being liked. I need to grapple and face up to this hard truth – some people will hate me simply because I love God. If we commit to live for the Lord Jesus in the Babylon of this 21st-century world, we have to accept that some people will react against us. Jesus himself warned us about this. Let's determine today not to let opposition or hostility throw us off course with our Lord, but to be women full of Christian integrity.

Dear Lord, please help me, like Daniel, live a life where the only charge people can bring against me has something to do with my love for God.

KATY JACK

A life regulated by prayer

Three times a day he got down on his knees and prayed, giving thanks to his God, just as he had done before. (NIV)

Flattery, a powerful lobby group, careless, shoddy drafting, a quick legislative process with no careful scrutiny – these things result in a new law entering the statute books, with disastrous consequences for God's people. Sound familiar? It's what happens in our passage today and increasingly it is what is happening in our own society. If laws are passed which put Christians in a difficult position, will we obey God and his revealed will in the Bible or will we obey the law of the land?

Darius' decree states that anyone who prayed to anyone other than him would be thrown into the lions' den. What will Daniel do? Lay off praying for a month? After all, it's only 30 days and God knows that he loves him and surely he wouldn't want Daniel to jeopardise his position in the court of the king?

Not a chance! Daniel learns of the new law and… goes to his room, faces Jerusalem and prays just as he has always done. His habit of prayer is such a part of his life that he can't just stop, even when threatened with the lions' den.

I stumbled across this quotation whilst preparing these studies: 'If your acts of prayer are the most regular thing in your life, I think you will be find they regulate everything else in your life.' My prayer life can feel so erratic. I long to be more like Daniel and have prayer regulate my life and not my life regulate my prayers.

Prayer got Daniel into a whole heap of trouble, and yet that very discipline of prayer and a lifetime of talking and walking with God enabled him to stand firm. It gave him courage, stability and, ultimately, wonderful protection as he bravely faced the lions' den.

What examples do you know of modern day 'Daniels'? Pray for those who dare to honour God in the face of serious opposition.

KATY JACK

Beasts in court

'As I looked, thrones were set in place, and the Ancient of Days took his seat… A river of fire was flowing, coming out from before him… The court was seated, and the books were opened. (NIV)

We are changing gear for our last four studies in Daniel, moving from historical accounts about life in the court of Babylon to the visions and dreams of Daniel about the court of heaven. It's as if God lifts back a veil and shows Daniel what is really going on behind the scenes in the heavenly realms.

This type of apocalyptic writing can seem confusing. There are lots of crazy images and vivid word pictures. We won't have time to delve into all the detail but there are some awesome truths to be mined here – so let's dig in!

Imagine that you are a film director and you are filming this chapter. The first scene with the four beasts requires some serious special effects! These four beasts rise out of the sea, symbolic in the Old Testament of chaos and evil. The lion with wings, the flesh-eating bear, the four-headed flying leopard sound terrifying. But the fourth beast is truly terrible. Many kings (horns) will come from this beast and the worst of them will seek to devour the earth and crush the people of God.

If this is all Daniel sees in his dream, he would have cause to be filled only with fear. Faced only with this scene, we would be left with no hope and only pessimism for the future.

But at verse 9, our director's camera sweeps into the throne room of heaven, where the Ancient of Days, God the Father, sits in glorious purity and holiness.

Meditate on this scene of the dazzling glory of God. He is the judge of all and, when his perfect timing is ready, he judges the beasts. Their power is taken away and they are destroyed. No fear or fuss. Just God being God.

Awesome God, thank you for the glimpse into your throne room. Please help me to remember that you are always in control and that nothing – no matter how wicked or powerful – can overcome you or your people.

KATY JACK

Reigning with the Son of Man

In my vision at night I looked, and there before me was one like a son of man, coming with the clouds of heaven. He approached the Ancient of Days and was led into his presence. (NIV)

From the churning sea and the throne room of heaven, the vision switches to the clouds of heaven as they deliver a new character. This son of man approaches the Ancient of Days and is brought into his presence, just like the beasts. How will this son of man be judged by the court of heaven? The beasts were stripped of their authority; the son of man is given authority, glory and sovereign power. The beasts devoured and trampled people; the son of man is worshipped by people from every nation and language. The fourth beast had his power taken away and was destroyed forever; the son of man's dominion is everlasting and his kingdom will never be destroyed. The beast oppressed the saints; the son of man shares the glory of his kingdom with the saints.

The son of man sounds wonderful, doesn't he?

'The Son of Man' was one of the names that Jesus used when talking about himself. When you consider all that Daniel's vision revealed about the son of man, that is pretty bold! Jesus was basically saying, 'I am the one to whom all authority, glory and power will one day be given.' How extraordinary, then, to consider that when he lovingly taught his disciples not to lord their power over others, he says 'even the Son of Man did not come to be served, but to serve, and to give his life as a ransom for many' (Mark 10:45).

Jesus, the Son of Man, gave up everything so that we could become people of God. He died so that we might live and reign with him in his perfect kingdom. What a joy it will be one day to be one of the multitude praising and worshipping Jesus, the Son of Man!

Dear Lord Jesus, thank you that even though you are the glorious Son of Man, you gave your life as a ransom for me.

KATY JACK

The reality of evil

He will cause deceit to prosper, and he will consider himself superior. When they feel secure, he will destroy many and take his stand against the Prince of princes. (NIV)

Rampaging rams and goats, big horns and little horns. This was one bonkers dream and it's not surprising that Daniel is left feeling exhausted by the end of it!

The ram and the goat in this vision are identified for us by Gabriel as the kings/kingdoms of Medes, Persia and Greece. Although the various horns growing out of the goat must have been a particularly surreal part of this dream, the description actually provides a good overview of the history of the Greek Empire. Alexander the Great established the Empire. After his death, it was divided amongst four of his generals, from whom arose Antiochus Epiphanes, a particular cruel persecutor of God's people.

Daniel is appalled by the vision. The glimpse into the future is terrifying – but it is also reassuring. God knows what the future holds. He knows all about Antiochus before the Greek Empire even exists. Nothing takes God by surprise.

And he doesn't want anything to take his people by surprise. The Bible is a totally honest book. God doesn't treat us like a toddler who needs to be protected from some of the scarier realities of life. He wants us to engage with the reality of evil. You don't send a soldier into battle without detailed knowledge of the enemy. And neither does God want his people living in the world naively optimistic about the inherent goodness of the world around us.

In one sense, there will always be rams and goats and horns terrorising the world. Many of our brothers and sisters in Christ are experiencing the full impact of being trampled by such beasts today. But wonderfully, as tomorrow's study shows, that is not the end of the story…

I pray for your people who are trampled by those who cause deceit to prosper and consider themselves superior to you. Please uphold them today and help them remember that the beast does not triumph in the end.

KATY JACK

The pattern and the promise

I am going to tell you what will happen later in the time of wrath, because the vision concerns the appointed time of the end. (NIV)

As we learned yesterday, this vision clearly relates to the Greek Empire. However, it also relates to the distant future, the appointed end of time. The message is one of hope to all God's people, living as exiles in Babylon throughout the ages. Words of comfort are given to Daniel by Gabriel. Look at the end of verse 25 – the evil one will be destroyed, but not by human power.

The pattern is clear – there will be beasts throughout the history of the world who seek to overthrow God and devour God's people.

The promise is wonderful – God will confront the beast. He will rescue his world and his people and establish his kingdom.

At the end of the Bible, Revelation picks up on the language and vision of Daniel. It describes the fall of Babylon, the destruction of the beast and the defeat of Satan. We don't know when it will happen, but the constant heartbeat of the Bible is that it will happen. We don't know when Jesus will return. Jesus himself said that he would come back like a thief in the night. He will return and establish his forever kingdom. That is certain.

Daniel is full of fear and confusion after the vision. But he then also shows great faith. He gets up and cracks on with the king's business.

God calls us to be like Daniel: to get up and live life to the full – not full of debilitating pessimism or unrealistic optimism, but trusting him, his plans and his timing. Keep your eyes fixed on that glorious day when the Son of Man is given all authority and the beast is defeated. Day by day, until he comes, let's keep following Daniel's example for living in Babylon – getting stuck in, drawing the line, speaking the truth, living boldly and praying constantly to our very great God.

Thank you, dear Lord Jesus, that you will return and that on that great day you will defeat Satan once and for all. Help me to live in the light of that hope and to stand firm for you in all that I do.

KATY JACK

Matthew's Gospel: Jesus teaches

Anne Calver writes:

We live in interesting times, don't we? There seems to be uncertainty and a sense of instability, brought on by terrorist attacks, government decisions, exiting the EU (for Britain) and the world economic climate. Coupled with this, there seem to be great divisions and disagreements in the church that threaten to tear us apart.

We can respond by retreating into the safety of our homes and churches in fear, or we can continue to advance the gospel in faith. No matter what we face, we are so blessed and now is the time to show that we follow a King who is over all kings and can equip us to stand through any trial.

Taking this into account, I have written studies based on Matthew's Gospel and the direct teachings of Jesus. Where better to go in a place of confusion than to the speaker of truth and life? He is clear what we shouldn't do: 'Do not worry' (6:25–34), 'Do not store up for yourselves treasure on earth' (6:19–24), 'Do not judge' (7:1–5) and do not conspicuously 'practise your righteousness in front of others' (6:1). Jesus also helps us to know what we should be doing: asking, seeking and knocking (7:7–12), building on a rock (7:24–27), praying (6:5–15), fasting (6:16–18), watching out for false prophets (7:15–16), producing good fruit (7:18–20) and continuing to go out to reach the lost (10:1–16). These truths help provide us with the template for life; they bring us freedom and security; and they help us to focus on Christ's mission rather than a broken world.

Recently, the Lord gave me a picture of person sitting in a chair. She was not moving. She was consuming, consuming, consuming to the point that she could not get out of the chair. I felt the Lord tell me that this is what the church can be like. I felt sick to the stomach. 'Lord, what do we need to do?' I cried out. My mind was taken to John 21, where Jesus reinstates Peter. Three times he says, 'Peter, do you really love me?' and Peter says, 'Yes, Lord.' Jesus replies, 'Feed my lambs.' As I reflected on the image of the person again, I felt God saying, 'Stop feeding yourself and start feeding others.'

Lord, help, equip and challenge us to be salt and light in a dark world for Jesus.

The tempter

Jesus said to him, 'Away from me, Satan! For it is written: "Worship the Lord your God and serve him only."' (NIV)

Temptation can be obvious: like a big bar of chocolate that you try desperately hard to resist, or an extra hour of TV when you know that you should be doing something else. Other temptations are not so clear and can be even more difficult to overcome. The enemy can cleverly cover up temptation, dressing it up in something 'godly' or 'acceptable'. You find yourself lured into walking down a road that feels right and that the world says is okay; but if pressed, you know it is not the way of the cross.

Satan encourages Jesus to prove his power, to exercise his dominion, promising more authority and greater influence. Status and pride are two things that tempt us towards taking power. However, Jesus does not give in to the words of the enemy. Of course he can turn stones to bread, throw himself down and be rescued, and take control of all kingdoms, but instead he declares the truth of scripture to silence Satan.

You wonder whether, in his human weakness, Jesus thought, 'Well, that's not a big deal, I can easily turn those stones to bread' – and yet he doesn't. He recognises the tempter at work; he sees through Satan's plan and does not give in.

Perhaps there are things in our lives that we are doing that seem acceptable to us, that the world says are okay and that make us feel 'good'. Could it be that the Lord is asking us to give those things up, to lay them down and to go another way? It may require humbling ourselves and doing something that other people won't understand or agree with, but it might just reveal more of Jesus to us and them.

'Enter through the narrow gate. For wide is the gate and broad is the road that leads to destruction, and many enter through it. But small is the gate and narrow the road that leads to life' (Matthew 7:13–14).

ANNE CALVER

The cost

'Come, follow me,' Jesus said, 'and I will send you out to fish for people.' At once they left their nets and followed him. (NIV)

So often I find myself calling to the children, 'Come on, kids, it's time to go!' – I find myself nagging them over and over again until I am literally shouting, 'Come ON, we have to leave NOW!' Sometimes it takes forever to get them out of the house or get them to do what I need them to do. One of the main reasons why I am there calling and waiting is that they think what they are doing is more important than what I am asking them to do.

When Jesus calls to Simon Peter and to Andrew, they are in the middle of casting their net into the lake – they are busy working as fishermen. And yet, we do not hear the brothers say, 'Wait a minute, this is more important, we need to finish the catch.' Instead, they leave their nets 'at once' to follow Jesus.

There is something about the call of Jesus that is so urgent and filled with such great authority that it doesn't matter what the disciples are doing; they know that going with this man is the better way. They are so convinced that they leave everything to follow him. Then, in the immediate verses that follow, James and John leave their nets and their *father* to follow Jesus.

Sometimes I wonder if I was there with the disciples, whether I would willingly leave everything, including family and income, to follow Jesus. Would I not be saying 'Wait a minute', just as my children do when I call, thinking my agenda was more important? Would we recognise his voice or be too busy? The disciples chose the most life-giving, amazing journey with Jesus; I pray that we can keep choosing life, too.

'Whether you turn to the right or to the left, your ears will hear a voice behind you, saying, "This is the way; walk in it." Then you will defile your idols overlaid with silver and images covered with gold' (Isaiah 30:21–22).

ANNE CALVER

The blessed

'Blessed are the pure in heart, for they will see God. Blessed are the peacemakers, for they will be called children of God.' (NIV)

Jesus climbs up the mountainside, sits down and begins to teach the crowd. Again and again, he talks to them about being blessed: blessed if they are poor in spirit, blessed if they mourn, blessed if they are meek, and so on. I have always found this a challenge to understand – by that, I mean that I know people who are mourning and they definitely don't feel blessed, and others who are poor in spirit (spiritually bankrupt), and do not feel blessed with the kingdom of heaven. The more I have looked at this, the more it became clear that Jesus wants those who are desperate for him to find in him all that they need.

Here in the sermon on the mount, Jesus uses the Greek word *makarios* in relation to blessing: having a self-contained happiness – knowing that we are fortunate, no matter what. The longing of our Lord in these verses is that our happiness should not be rooted in our circumstances, but in knowing him. The blessing is in being followers of Christ, not in what is happening in our lives.

I remember meeting a woman who had been in solitary confinement for her faith in Jesus. When she came out of prison after three months, she went and planted another church, even though she knew she could be arrested again. This woman shone with the love of God; she radiated an infectious passion for Christ. She knew what it was to hunger and thirst, to mourn, to long for peace, to be persecuted and yet she knew she was blessed. Meeting this woman challenged me to pursue becoming a woman of purity, to seek peace and hunger for righteousness, so that I might see and know God more.

Are you blessed? In what ways? Why not spend time thanking Jesus for all that he has done for you and asking him that you might know that self-contained happiness, despite your circumstances.

ANNE CALVER

The light of love

'In the same way let your light shine before others, that they may see your good deeds and praise your Father in heaven.' (NIV)

We have some new friends who, when I read this passage, truly seem to sum up what it means to love your neighbour and let your light shine before others. How? They genuinely don't keep the love of Jesus to themselves. They do not use church as a bowl to hide under, or their house as a haven to escape their noisy neighbours. Every week, they invite people into their world and enter theirs, too. I have not known them come to church without bringing others with them. They seek to love their neighbours through genuine hospitality and pray faithfully that they can demonstrate the love of God to those they come into contact with.

I sometimes wonder if our lives are just so busy with work that relationships get pushed on to the back burner. Maybe our time is spent 'doing' and we forget about 'being'. The words of Jesus to Mary and Martha in Luke 10 challenge deeply – are we at the feet of Jesus listening to what he is saying? Are we so busy rushing about that we forget about listening to him and listening to others?

These two passages talk about loving, praying, shining and serving others. I know so often I am making 'me' the focus of these things because of the busyness of life. Have you lost your saltiness? What flavour do you bring to the people that you see? Jesus wants to meet with you, restoring and refreshing you by the power of his Holy Spirit.

Lord, show us how to slow, how to seek, how to serve – not striving but surrendering – so that we are salt and light in a dark and lost world. Fill our hearts with the love of Jesus so that it overflows to those we meet.

ANNE CALVER

The way to pray

'This then is how you should pray: "Our Father in heaven, hallowed be your name, your Kingdom come, your will be done on earth as it is in heaven."' (NIV)

A short time ago, I read some really helpful notes in relation to the Lord's Prayer. Mike Breen's *Building a Discipling Culture* (2014) encourages readers to pray through the lines of the Lord's Prayer, giving space to add words from your heart. I began to jog a few years ago and pray these words: 'My Father in heaven, hallowed be your name', continuing further with words like 'Lord, I worship you, I praise you, God of eternity, God over everything – you are awesome, you are holy. I love you.' Then I'd leave a few moments before moving on to the next line of the Lord's Prayer found in today's reading. By the end of the prayer, I had been able to get my heart and conscience clear before the king, ask for the things that were on my mind, lay down the worries and pray for protection over those I love. I also found that I hadn't just prayed for my little world, but had reflected on the bigger, wider needs in the world. No wonder Jesus says 'this then is how you should pray' (v. 9).

Recently, the world has seemed to be consumed with issues: ongoing terror atrocities, government complexities and pain and heartache felt by those we love. The line 'Let your will be done' has become one of the only ways I know how to pray. 'Lord, we have no answers, we cannot make everything okay, and so please, Lord, will you intervene and have your way. Let your will be done, not ours.'

God isn't asking us for big words and clear sentences; he just longs to hear our cries and know our hearts. Turn to him today and, even if you only have the strength to utter 'Jesus', he will draw close.

'Be still, and know that I am God; I will be exalted among the nations, I will be exalted in the earth' (Psalm 46:10).

ANNE CALVER

The secret place

'Then your Father, who sees what is done in secret, will reward you.'
(NIV)

As a child I was led to believe that secrets were not a good thing. If you whispered a secret in someone's ear, it made other people feel left out and unhappy. If you were told to keep a secret, it would eventually come out into the open and people would be upset that you didn't tell them earlier.

We all know that some things done in secret are not good for us and can cause a lot of pain. 2 Corinthians 4:2 says, 'Rather, we have renounced secret and shameful ways; we do not use deception, nor do we distort the word of God.'

My mum would always encourage honesty and openness and every time I kept something from her, it would hurt her and it would hurt me. However, Jesus is clear that there are some things that we should do in secret, things that we do not need to discuss with everyone. He encourages giving in secret (v. 4) and fasting in secret (vv. 17–18). We do not need to make a big song and dance out of giving to others; we just give quietly. We don't give to get back; we just give freely and, if possible, in secret. Jesus knows that giving and fasting are costly to us, but he will reward us. We don't need the world's 'Well done'.

My husband Gavin and I were eating in a restaurant a short time ago and we came to pay the bill, only to discover that someone had paid for everything we had eaten! At first I felt bad, because we had had at least two courses! However, we left the place feeling so blessed and encouraged. We had no idea who gave us the meal but I know Jesus will reward them.

Have you ever given in secret? How did it feel? Did you get to see how the person responded? Why not try giving quietly and generously this week in a way you never have before?

ANNE CALVER

The real treasure

'Do not store up for yourselves treasures on earth, where moths and vermin destroy, and where thieves break in and steal. But store up for yourselves treasures in heaven.' (NIV)

I vividly remember how the Lord began to unsettle us in our comfortable house in the Midlands and lead me to being willing to move to London. We sold the house in just four days, and very quickly I found myself packing boxes. As I began to go through piles of clothes, I found that my eyes were filling with tears; yes, I was sad to be leaving, but I was crying for a different reason. I was appalled by how many things there were on the floor in front of me, saddened by how many boxes we needed for our 'treasure'. There were items that came out of the cupboards that we didn't even know we had – what then was the point of having them?

The Lord really stirred my heart that day and in the end we took a lot fewer boxes down to London than I had anticipated. Our moving was also at a time when the news was broadcasting images of millions of refugees fleeing for their lives with only the shirt on their back. How could I justify all this earthly treasure? Since the move, we have tried to keep from filling every nook and cranny with bits that we do not need and, even more than that, be attentive to the Lord in what we say we 'need' and what we can live without. We haven't mastered it yet!

I believe the Lord Jesus is calling us to focus on his will, his kingdom, his plans, more than we focus on the material goods that surround and tempt us. Will we put a house, job, money, and so on ahead of seeking his will for our lives? So challenging. What are we prepared to give up, hold lightly, to see what he will do?.

'Then Jesus said to his disciples, "Truly I tell you… it is easier for a camel to go through the eye of a needle than for a rich man to enter the kingdom of God."' (Matthew 19:23–24).

ANNE CALVER

The worrier

'Therefore do not worry about tomorrow, for tomorrow will worry about itself. Each day has enough trouble of its own.' (NIV)

I cannot count the number of times that I have heard my husband say to me, 'Just don't worry, Anne. The Bible says not to worry; trust God.' Sometimes these words have made me want to wring his neck! Anyone who worries knows that it is easier said than done to just 'stop worrying'. The truth is that some of us are more inclined to feeling worried or anxious than others, and I definitely envy those who are laid back.

These words in Matthew are deeply challenging. Who of us can add a single hour to our life by worrying? (v. 27).

At 'Mums and Tots' today, one of the grannies who was looking after her grandchildren commented to me, 'Now I have raised my own children, I wish I could say to my old self, "Stop worrying about where they will go to preschool or who they play with or what you are getting right and wrong, because they will turn out fine. They will all be okay."'

I think some of our worrying is a lack of trust in God. Will he really provide? Will he really come through for my family? I love that open question right in the middle of the passage: 'Are you not much more valuable than [the birds]?' (v. 26). The more we realise how valuable we are, the less we worry.

As we seek and receive his love, we gradually begin to find rest in the knowledge of that love. When I worry, it is because somehow it feels as though I have to control and manage my life. The fact is our lives belong to our maker and he wants us to surrender our concerns to him, asking him to bring us his peace.

'My help comes from the Lord, the maker of heaven and earth. He will not let your foot slip – he who watches over you will not slumber; indeed, he who watches over Israel will neither slumber nor sleep' (Psalm 121:2–4).

ANNE CALVER

The plank in our eye

'Why do you look at the speck of sawdust in your brother's eye and pay
no attention to the plank in your own eye?... Take out the plank from
your own eye, and then you will see clearly to remove the speck from
your brother's eye.' (NIV)

Have you ever felt judged? How did it make you feel?

When I have sensed judgement in some way, it has made me cross
and I want to back away from the person who is judging me. One of the
biggest reactions in my heart has been, 'How dare they judge me, when
they are behaving like that!' Judging someone is so easy to do: a person
passes us in the street and we can make very quick judgements about
them; a member of our family decides to date someone that we don't like
and we pass all kinds of judgements on the relationship. We judge people
based on the decisions that they make, the friendships they hold and the
way that they choose to live. Sadly, some of these judgements are made
with very little understanding. This quotation is helpful: 'Be careful how
you judge people; you don't sum up a person's life in one moment' (Al
Pacino in *City Hall*).

The problem is that we can get these words of Jesus mixed up. He is
not saying ignore all bad choices that are being made or let people continue in a life of sin. He is addressing our hearts and our spirits first. If we
help someone to discern truth and walk away from error by offering wisdom with the right motive, that is not judgement.

The question is: have we addressed the plank in our own eye? Are we
seeking to be transformed by the Lord? Because a blind guide cannot lead
a partially sighted person. Jesus says, 'If a blind man leads a blind man,
both will fall into a pit' (Matthew 15:14). Only if we see well ourselves can
we help others to see, too. Love has to be the motivator in all things.

Father, help me to love you with all my heart, soul, mind and strength.
Please transform me so that I can partner with you in loving others and
seeing lives changed. Let me be motivated by your compassion.

ANNE CALVER

The door

'Ask and it will be given to you; seek and you will find; knock and the door will be opened to you. For everyone who asks receives; the one who seeks finds; and to the one who knocks, the door will be opened.' (NIV)

If you asked my seven-year-old to interpret these words in Matthew 7, he would be very excited. 'Mummy, does that mean that I can have whatever I ask for, and go and do whatever I want?' I can hear his longings in my ear! And my response: 'No, son, that would not be good for you and that is not what Jesus is trying to say!' Tears and a hung head would then be the order of the day.

The truth is that Jesus is talking more about prayer: persevering with prayer and getting to know him. The more we seek first his kingdom, the more we will find and receive the things that he is longs to give to his children. Not gifts of gold, frankincense and myrrh, but spiritual gifts from his throne room to equip us to know his love and to serve and bless others.

Jesus is longing for us not just to use words (ask) or our minds (seek) but to take action (knock) as well. He wants us to pursue him with the right motives, to put him and his will ahead of everything else and to enter into a relationship with him. We don't ask, seek and knock just once. We keep coming to Jesus asking, seeking and knocking for others as well as for ourselves so that we can see him open doors for them, too. After all, he stands at the door knocking from the other side and he longs to come in and eat with us (Revelation 3:20).

I love the way Jesus says, '*How much more* will your Father in heaven give good gifts' (v. 11). There is more power, more love, more freedom, more intimacy, more wisdom and more understanding for all of us when we keep asking, seeking and knocking.

Is there something about which the Lord is calling you to ask, seek and knock? Perhaps you have even stopped praying about it, but he longs for you to come to him afresh with your burdens today.

ANNE CALVER

The narrow gate

'Enter through the narrow gate. For wide is the gate and broad is the road that leads to destruction, and many enter through it.' (NIV)

When you think about surrendering your life to Jesus, it doesn't seem too difficult: say sorry for your sin, thank him for his sacrifice and invite him to live and reign in your heart. However, *living* as a Christian in the way that Jesus was calling his followers to is not simple.

I remember when my husband Gavin and I wanted to move house, but we could not sell our property. We were a bit bored, looking for a new challenge and moving to a bigger home in a nice location seemed sensible. However, after pushing the door for nearly a year, we realised that we were not on the right road – it was an agenda that we were humanly wanting and pushing for when the narrow gate meant sitting still and waiting for the Lord to lead the way. Taking the house off the market was difficult to do, but we would have never found the church that we then settled in, and I know that bit of the journey was a key part of the road to life.

I am sure Jesus is talking again of the narrow road in Luke, when he talks to three people about the cost of following him (Luke 9:57–62). One of them says, 'I will follow you wherever you go' and you then expect Jesus to say, 'Brilliant, come.' Instead, he reminds the person that he has no place to lay his head. To the other two, he makes it plain that to follow him means laying other things down and placing him first. Going the narrow way is costly and challenging, but it leads to greater intimacy with the king; it leads us to a place of living life in all its fullness.

What do you love about your life? Are there things that you hold tightly to and would never want to give up in order to follow Jesus? Ask him to reveal the narrow way more to you today.

ANNE CALVER

The false prophets

'Watch out for false prophets. They come to you in sheep's clothing, but inwardly they are ferocious wolves. By their fruit you will recognise them.' (NIV)

'Mummy, why do you wear make-up?' came the inquiring voice of my ten-year-old daughter as I was hastily dabbing mascara on before the school run. 'Well, because I like it,' I responded. 'You don't need it, Mummy, you are beautiful anyway,' she declared. I grabbed her and gave her the biggest hug! 'Thank you, sweetie,' I whispered into her ear. This interaction made me think about what I was 'putting on' in terms of make-up and clothes, and why I did it. We can all dress the part, can't we? The question is – are we hiding from who we really are?

Jesus says that we might be outwardly looking the part in our sheep's clothing, but are we the same inwardly? Are we really who we appear to be? We should aim to be lovers of Jesus inside and out: not people who just say we are Christians, but who live like Jesus and are being transformed bit by bit, day by day.

A man or woman may be dressed in ministerial garb and accorded all the dignity of church office, but is he or she committed to following Christ? Jesus says, 'By their fruit you will know them… A bad tree cannot bear good fruit' (vv. 17–18). What we wear, what we say and what we do is not what makes us followers of Jesus; it is our relationship with him that is truly important.

Do we really know him? I don't know about you, but I do not want to face Jesus for him to say, 'I never knew you' (v. 23) and I want to affect lives according to his will, not my own. The sermon on the mount has a deep call: to stop working on the outward appearance and seek intimacy and transformation at the feet of Jesus.

'I am the vine; you are the branches. If you remain in me and I in you, you will bear much fruit; apart from me you can do nothing' (John 15:5).

ANNE CALVER

The wise and foolish builders

'Therefore everyone who hears these words of mine and puts them into practice is like a wise man who built his house on the rock.' (NIV)

Recently, a primary school near us was closed down. There was no advance warning to parents and all of them had to work out quickly where they were going to relocate the kids. All the schools in the area are at capacity so the majority of children are now travelling miles to be educated, in a community that is not their own. The reason for closure: they discovered that the school had been built over a sinkhole and bit by bit the classrooms were beginning to subside.

The school looked perfect externally, but little did they realise what they had been building on.

What are you building on? There is such a Western culture 'pull' to build our lives on getting a good job, buying a house and a car, and getting the most recent gadgets to keep ourselves 'on trend'. There is also, for some of us, an unconscious tendency to base our lives on how our parents raised us – we find ourselves mirroring the way that they lived. None of these things may be bad, but are they what drive our decisions?

There's a great quotation that my brother-in-law used to have on a T-shirt: 'He who dies with the most toys, still dies.' Money, houses, cars, jobs, status, etc. is all sand, and if our life is built on those things it could come crashing down. To build on 'rock', we make Jesus our number-one priority: we get to know him and his will for our lives and we make decisions based on what we believe he would do. Then, even if something falls, we keep standing, and we trust in him.

'And I tell you that you are Peter, and on this rock I will build my church' (Matthew 16:18). If we build on rock, we become like rock and Jesus can then use us to do great things for him.

ANNE CALVER

The twelve

'I am sending you out like sheep among wolves. Therefore be as shrewd as snakes and as innocent as doves.' (NIV)

Jesus calls the twelve to him and 'gives them authority' (v. 1). He doesn't just send them out as sheep into wolf territory; he gives them his authority from heaven. Then later, we see that the authority extends to all believers, when the Holy Spirit comes and the disciples are empowered.

I believe the Lord is calling us to come to Jesus again, to be filled afresh with the power of the Holy Spirit, so that his authority is conferred upon us and lives are transformed. A short time ago, I felt the Lord put these words in my heart: 'My child, I am raising up an army. I am not raising up soldiers that carry weapons of destruction, that hold in their hands clubs and knives. I am raising up an army whose weapons are my word and Spirit.'

In my mind, I saw a man sharpening swords and felt the Lord was saying, 'I am sharpening my people. I am sharpening the tools in their hands, so that the truth can cut deep into the hearts of many.'

I saw a child's face and the light from a huge flaming torch came near and lit up her face. I felt the Lord say, 'My royal priesthood, my holy nation, are being set apart. I am setting their faces like flint to walk into the darkness.' Then I saw a huge procession of people carrying these flame torches through the night. 'Not by might, nor by power, but by my Spirit,' said the Lord. By his Holy Spirit, he will shine on those living in darkness.

God is raising up his army, an army prepared to lay down the ways of the world, and follow the way of the Spirit.

If we are sent out, we need to get ready. To be prepared means that we get ready in advance. Do you want to be part of this army and see God's kingdom come in your area?

ANNE CALVER

The proverbial woman

Michele D. Morrison writes:

Many Facebook posts I see consist of modern proverbs dollied up in attractive poster styles. Not all of them are wise. 'Everything happens for a reason.' 'If it feels good, do it.' Really? Over the next fortnight, we're going to look at God's words of wisdom. We're told in 2 Chronicles 1 that, after a costly sacrifice, Solomon asked to hear from God. God invited him to ask for whatever he wanted, and he asked for wisdom, and was given it (though his later accumulation of thousands of concubines revealed that a streak of folly still ran through him). In the book of Proverbs, he passes on godly advice to his son.

We are looking in particular at the words of wisdom pertaining to women. Some proverbs refer to wives or mothers but, in fact, the truths are applicable to all women, sometimes to humanity in general, and they are not restricted to women in partnerships or to parents.

Eugene Peterson calls Proverbs 'a manual for living'. 'Tune your ears to the world of Wisdom; set your heart on a life of Understanding… If you make Insight your priority… before you know it Fear-of-God will be yours; you'll have come upon the Knowledge of God' (Proverbs 2:2–5, MSG).

I did not expect to encounter the concept of the fear of the Lord so frequently as I did. Solomon teaches that the fear of God means hating evil, enables skilled living, expands life, builds up confidence, is a spring of living water, teaches humility, is life itself, gives a full and satisfying life, is your future – and when you know the fear of the Lord, you experience God's glory.

These ideas weave through Proverbs like a golden thread and provide the backdrop for so much of the teaching on how the wise woman ought to carry herself.

I have learned a lot as I have been challenged, encouraged and chastised reading through these proverbs again and again. May you be blessed as you journey with me over these next days, leap-frogging through the bulk of the book before landing on the renowned Proverbs 31 woman.

Together, we discover that the glory of Proverbs 31 is not that one woman accomplished all these amazing things, but that God is delighted to throw wide the doors of opportunity to all women and beckons us to step out, boldly and wisely, in the fear of the Lord.

Dream team

Listen, my son, to your father's instruction and do not forsake your mother's teaching. They are a garland to grace your head and a chain to adorn your neck. (NIV)

Solomon gravely instructs his son to heed the teaching of both male and female role models in his home. He describes a dream team, father and mother, whose teachings (and exemplary lives) together offer a child a healthy start in life. The mother's teaching is as valuable as the father's – no gender bias here.

In reality, though, not every father and mother make a dream team; even the best parents fall short at times. Many children are deprived of good role models in their families, and society often celebrates men and women whose values and conduct are not what God would want children to mimic. We Christian women should celebrate and share the testimonies of those in the public eye who do exemplify the best and who live by God's standards.

As the African saying goes, 'It takes a village to raise a child.' As Christian women – whether or not we are mothers – we have a responsibility to teach God's values. We teach by word and we teach by example to all children in our circle, whether they are our own children, nieces and nephews, or children in the neighbourhood, the congregation, schools or voluntary organisations.

Although Solomon instructs his son to value the teaching he gets in the home, in verse 7 he draws attention to the best teacher and the most valuable knowledge: 'The fear of the Lord is the beginning of knowledge.' True knowledge springs from our relationship with God the Father; the deeper, more alive our relationship is, the more we will revere him and be open to receiving his mind and his thoughts and living his way.

Obedience to God is the source of true beauty, adorning us with everlasting garlands and breath-taking necklaces which identify us as family and attract others to God.

Teach us the fear of the Lord, Father, so that we might pass on this knowledge to the next generation. May our words and our lives inspire others, as we remain in you.

MICHELE D. MORRISON

Dame Wisdom

Out in the open wisdom calls aloud, she raises her voice in the public squares; on top of the wall she cries out, at the city gate she makes her speech. (NIV)

Here we meet Dame Wisdom. It's tempting to conclude that wisdom is female, but it's just syntax: the gender of the Hebrew noun is feminine! (Yet the fact that this patriarchal society chose to make this word – representing a crucial concept in God's eyes – feminine suggests an ancient respect for women which is often overlooked.)

Some people identify Wisdom as Jesus, and certainly he personified wisdom while he lived on earth. He only did what he saw his Father in heaven doing (John 5:19). He acted and spoke the words of God, not presuming to be independently wise; his humility, actions and words sprang from that loving relationship which recognised the awesomeness of the Father, and respected him with a holy fear.

I find it interesting that wisdom here is not found in solitary contemplation in the barrenness of a desert, nor in cloistered isolation with other meditative types – though no doubt wisdom is in these places, too. Here though, she is vocal, crying out in the busiest parts of town – in the noisy streets and the gateways and public squares. Perhaps the busiest parts of town today are on social media.

Can you think of creative ways to subtly reveal your faith on Twitter or Facebook? The internet and TV host many fools who promote shallow lives lacking the moral compass only a relationship with God can give. Can we counter this somehow? The world is in a mess, and the only one who can create order out of the chaos is God. We believers – women and men – must upload our voices to the public platforms, be that on social media, the printed page or simply by 'gossiping God' to our neighbours and friends.

Lord Jesus, fill me again today with your Holy Spirit, so that your wisdom lives in me. Give me courage to speak truth in love into every situation I encounter today.

MICHELE D. MORRISON

Sin City

Say to wisdom, 'You are my sister,' and to insight, 'You are my relative.' They will keep you from the adulterous woman, from the wayward woman with her seductive words. (NIV)

The fear of the Lord is the beginning of wisdom, and respect develops as we press in to know God intimately as our loving Father. Here wisdom is called 'sister' and understanding 'relative': the language of family.

Temptation is personified as the woman who betrays her vows in order to satisfy her lust. Solomon was writing to his son; had he been writing to his daughter, he might have warned her to beware the man who betrays his vows in order to satisfy his lust. Broken promises of the most intimate, heart-rending kind, tearing apart couples and often bereaving children of one of their parents, stranding them in a bobbing sea of insecurity: adultery is deadly. Yet it is a routine plot line in films and TV shows, and often a device for comedy. But there is nothing funny about a broken marriage.

In this post-truth era, vows are taken lightly, be they vows to each other or vows to God. God hates that. Our word should be our bond. We should have high standards.

Faithful monogamy is a challenge in today's society, where sexual appetites for all sorts of combinations are condoned. As church and as individuals, we are called to holiness, which finds its source in the fear of the Lord.

When we stick close to wisdom (to God), we will recognise temptation for what it is. Our respect for God will give us courage and strength to resist becoming a temptress or falling prey to a tempter.

Sin is sin, but there is something especially heartbreaking about sexual sin. The church is called the bride of Christ, and the book of Hosea uses sexual infidelity to illustrate the broken covenant between the Israelites and God. It is a broken promise which cuts to the core.

Our relationship with God should eclipse the attractions of all other idols. God is always ready to meet us at the trysting place; are you ready to meet him?

MICHELE D. MORRISON

R-E-S-P-E-C-T

A kind-hearted woman gains honour, but ruthless men gain only wealth. (NIV)

Aretha Franklin belted it out in the '60s. R-E-S-P-E-C-T. My husband Don went to boarding school, and was once berated by a 'master' for not showing him enough respect. Don's response was that respect has to be earned. (I think that conclusion earned him another beating!)

This proverb of Solomon's suggests that respect can be gained through kindness, but this isn't about acts of kindness; the proverb goes right to the state of the heart, because the state of one's heart affects everything we are.

So how do we become kind-hearted, or as in *The Message*, 'women of gentle grace'?

When Christ transforms our hearts, he enables us to live lives of natural integrity: attitudes and actions are joined up and, because Jesus empowers us, we are new creations. This doesn't mean our every attitude will be inspired by kindness once the Holy Spirit lives in our hearts. We are works in progress, as they say, and kindness may not be our natural, default reaction to adverse situations or contrary people. We have to be willing to be changed, and then he can change us.

The second part of the verse concludes that ruthlessness gains 'only' wealth. In this materialistic world, a big bank account is for many people a noble goal. A B&B guest told me that, because her son had the money to purchase a house, he had 'done good'. This is a seductive lie. A lifestyle of conspicuous consumption, notoriety, fame: the 'respect' these things earn us is shallow and illusory.

All around us are people lost in a dark world, straining to see the light. A smile, a helping hand, or a gentle word restores hope and peace in a world in turmoil and gives others a glimpse of God's glory.

Lord of all wisdom, give me vision, wisdom and a heart open to receive you, so that your kindness can flow through me and into a harsh world. May I be a woman of gentle grace.

MICHELE D. MORRISON

Grunting

Like a gold ring in a pig's snout is a beautiful woman who shows no discretion. (NIV)

Like a gold ring in a pig's snout is a beautiful face on an empty head. (MSG)

Because God proscribed pork from the Jewish diet, pigs were detestable to the Israelites. The idea of adorning an unclean animal with a beautiful gold ring is perhaps funny to us, but would have been shocking to Solomon's son. This is a vibrant, offensive image. A pig's snout digs the dirt, or worse. A gold ring there would pick up detritus and quickly lose its beauty. I imagine it would interfere with the pig's dig. It might impair her breathing. It certainly would not enhance her appearance.

I leafed through a magazine at the hairdresser's, noting that some dresses worn to events by the beautiful women of the world are becoming like the 'emperor's new clothes'. Various movie stars and singers, young and old, model see-through dresses or even strings of crystal beads with skimpy underwear distinctly visible. Some discretion lacking, perhaps?

Discretion is not limited to the way we dress, but is perhaps more a mark of behaviour. To be discreetly generous, for example, is beautiful; to tweet your generosity tarnishes it.

Jesus pointed out the poor widow who quietly gave everything she had and trusted God for future provision. He contrasted her love and generosity with the rich Pharisees who ostentatiously threw their offerings into the pots so that the noise could echo round the temple and proclaim their generosity to everyone. Crass: a gold ring in a pig's snout.

Beauty germinates in the heart, and blossoms into attitudes and actions of fragrant kindness.

Lord, give me wisdom as I choose my wardrobe and jewellery. Help me to dress in such a way that it's my heart which is striking, and your glory can be seen in all I am.

MICHELE D. MORRISON

Build on the rock

The wise woman builds her house, but with her own hands the foolish one tears hers down. (NIV)

Lives of careless wrongdoing are tumbledown shacks; holy living builds soaring cathedrals. (MSG)

My three-year-old granddaughter's favourite story is the Three Little Pigs. In the story, only the well-built brick house can withstand the vicious attack of the Big Bad Wolf.

Solomon advises us to use the best building materials when constructing our lives. Those materials are found in the Bible. When we study the blueprint for building a successful life and then, with God's help, seek to follow it, we build lives that can withstand the attacks of the enemy.

Our enemy is no fairy-tale villain. His breath fans the embers of hurt until they glow with resentment and flare into anger, destroying relationships, disrupting families, devouring faith and leaving us desolate.

Our enemy is no fairy-tale villain. He seeks out our vulnerabilities and delights to find our deepest hurts, huffing doubt into someone's mind, puffing rejection into someone's heart, seeking to bring down all that would glorify and celebrate our Saviour.

Our enemy is no fairy-tale villain. He loves to make us affronted when disappointed by someone, consuming relationships, consuming us.

Forgiveness is the water for dousing the flames of disappointment and hurt, of anger and resentment.

When the enemy seeks to invade our lives, sliding down into our hearts, we can destroy him by stoking the hot fires of faith, consuming him in the word of God, the presence of Jesus and the power of the Holy Spirit. We are safe in Jesus, but we are still vulnerable to attack. Don't be fooled by the enemy, and tear your house down because the fire of faith has burned low.

Who's afraid of the Big Bad Wolf? When our lives are built on Jesus, though the enemy may huff, and he may puff, he can't blow us down.

Lord Jesus, help me to build my house on you, the rock of ages, so that no storm, no attack of the enemy, will undermine me.

MICHELE D. MORRISON

Nag, nag, nag

A quarrelsome wife is like the dripping of a leaky roof in a rainstorm; restraining her is like restraining the wind or grasping oil with the hand. (NIV)

Again, I'm going to claim the universality of the wisdom of this proverb, which is not limited to wives, nor to women, but to humanity in general. We all have days when we are irritable, but this proverb describes one who has allowed irritability to take root and become a defining characteristic of her personality. The principle is repeated in many proverbs: 19:13, 21:9 and 25:24.

So why does God so roundly condemn argumentativeness? It kills relationships; it wounds the spirit; and it drains life of spontaneous beauty and joy. An argumentative spirit is conceived in pride, betraying a superior attitude or a suspicious defensiveness. It discourages dialogue and compromise, and stifles wisdom. Civilised dialogue allows wisdom to bubble through conversations, but opinionated and aggressive words carve deep chasms in relationships and can severely undermine the self-esteem of those on the receiving end of criticism. There remain no foundations on which to bridge the gap.

Recently, we had a couple stay with us at our B&B for a fortnight. The first night, they expressed views we found shocking. God muted us and, as the days passed, they shared the profound hurts which prompted their opinions. Compassion replaced disgust. Had we argued that first night, a quarrelsome spirit could have denied us a glimpse into their life journeys. We'd never have understood them. We are the richer for the experience.

'To answer before listening – that is folly and shame' (Proverbs 18:13). A person with a quarrelsome nature doesn't listen.

Though this proverb reaches a pessimistic conclusion, in Christ, there is always hope: hope for change, hope that, though it is like restraining the wind, Jesus is Lord over the wind. If you or a friend or partner has a quarrelsome nature, take it to the Lord in prayer.

Heavenly Father, I am aware that at times my spirit is pinched and mean, and I humbly open myself to your Spirit now to change me.

MICHELE D. MORRISON

Crown him

A wife of noble character is her husband's crown, but a disgraceful wife is like decay in his bones. (NIV)

Not everyone reading these notes is a wife, but the teaching is applicable to us all because the church is the bride of Christ. We are meant to be church in such a way that Christ is crowned in glory. So how do we demonstrate nobility of character as church? In Micah 6:8 (MSG), God says, 'It's quite simple: do what is fair and just to your neighbour, be compassionate and loyal in your love, and don't take yourself too seriously – take God seriously.'

Take God seriously. The fear of the Lord is the beginning of wisdom.

The aim of a noble person is to achieve excellence in character, not accolades in society. Some people aspire to fame and fortune and, with the proliferation of reality TV programmes, there are many shooting stars who flare and quickly die out. Our aspiration should be to lift Jesus higher, individually and as church. We need to take God seriously.

Jesus set out a challenging manifesto in his sermon on the mount (Matthew 5—7). It is a countercultural recipe for living a noble life which achieves joy, satisfaction and spiritual rewards. Matthew 5:9 says: 'Blessed are the peacemakers, for they will be called children of God' (NIV); 'You're blessed when you can show people how to cooperate instead of compete or fight. That's when you discover who you really are, and your place in God's family' (MSG).

Are you a peacemaker? Is your church a blessing to your community? Are your doors open to the homeless? Are your ears open to those suffering injustice? Are your arms open to the lonely? Are your purses open to the poor? Are you spreading a table and inviting everyone to enjoy the Lord's hospitality through you?

Father God, purify my heart that I may be as gold to you. Fill me with your Spirit, Jesus. Pour out your Spirit on your church, so that we might fashion a crown of glory for you.

MICHELE D. MORRISON

The ripple effect

Her children arise and call her blessed; her husband also, and he praises her: 'Many women do noble things, but you surpass them all.' (NIV)

The effect of nobility is not confined to a home, but ripples through a community or a workplace. 'Noble' is defined in the dictionary as: magnanimous, a courageous spirit and generosity of mind.

My mother showed nobility when I married a Scot and moved 6,000 miles from her. Now that my own children are making similar decisions, I am struggling to take inspiration from her and strength from the Lord. I, too, want to be noble.

One doesn't do noble things with an eye to a reward, but neither does one do them in a vacuum. Nobility affects others. It encourages others to be better themselves. It lifts others' eyes from the routine and opens up a vista of possibilities. This passage praises the woman for bringing good, not harm, to those closest to her.

Nobility is more than an action; it's an attitude. It flows from the inside out, finding its source in the innermost being, bubbling up in the heart. Jesus taught, 'It's your heart, not the dictionary, that gives meaning to your words. A good person produces good deeds and words season after season' (Matthew 12:34–35, MSG).

Season after season, in summer and in winter, in joy and in sorrow. There is a consistency about nobility. It doesn't just flash out on occasion before settling back into ordinariness. Depending on the translation used, this exemplary woman is more precious than diamonds or rubies – precious gems, created under pressure and over time. Someone once described faith as a long walk in the same direction. It's on that journey that nobility emerges, and none of us can be noble on our own. Partnering with the Spirit of Jesus, though, we can become less so that he becomes more, and his true nobility shines from our lives.

O Lord, birth nobility in me today. May my heart's desires be your heart's desires, so that I bring blessing and honour to those around me, and glory to your name.

MICHELE D. MORRISON

Open heart, open purse

**She's quick to assist anyone in need, reaches out to help the poor.
(MSG)**

Spontaneous generosity and compassion characterise this woman. She opens her arms to the poor; because she is industrious, she has more than she needs and wants to share.

In the days of Solomon, I would imagine that the only needy folk this woman encountered were those on her doorstep or en route to market. I find it challenging to identify which needs my husband and I should try to meet. Today, we debated whether to send support to a young woman who is doing amazing work among undocumented workers north of Seattle, and/or to give a donation to a young woman from our congregation who is doing outreach work in a local university. Or should our limited resources go to famine victims or refugees, the persecuted church or political action lobbyists, the homeless or medical research charities, or…? The list of needs is endless and heartbreaking.

Jesus counselled us not to be naive. We have to be wise but also generous. Those of us blessed with resources are called to open our arms quickly and cheerfully. Some refugee families from the Middle East conflicts have moved into a town near us. It didn't take much trouble to connect with them and draw them into a network of folk who are ready and willing to help. The refugees are being assisted by the local authority, but there are things they need and we are part of a giving church which sees itself as a 'blessing machine'. The real help they crave is to improve their English, and to do that they want visitors to spend time with them, speaking English. Often the most sacrificial gift we can give is of our time, of ourselves.

Where is God challenging you? Do you have a prayerful strategy for giving or do you respond emotionally? As we open our hands, our hearts grow.
                                                    MICHELE D. MORRISON

A woman of the world

She gets up while it is still dark; she provides food for her family and portions for her servant girls. She considers a field and buys it; out of her earnings she plants a vineyard. (NIV)

The old stereotypical image of the ideal Christian woman as one whose role is restricted to homemaking is blown apart by this portrait of a very industrious and shrewd businesswoman. Her success combines her business skills with sheer hard work. She's up before dawn and works on after dark, busy with both domestic chores and business decisions. One wonders what is left for her husband to do except swan around looking splendid at the city gates!

The cloistering and minimising of women's opportunities in some Christian traditions seems to deny the breadth of skills this woman demonstrates. In truth, few woman are going to be blessed with so many talents, but the fact that they are lauded here validates them as possibilities for women's aspirations. The world is the poorer for the denial of opportunities extended to women in various cultures, at various times and even today.

In Philippi, Paul evangelised Lydia, who worked as a successful businesswoman trading in purple cloth – an expensive commodity. Priscilla worked alongside her husband making tents. Multitasking, realising potential outside the home as well as within it, has a long history.

Though the proliferation of so many gifts apparent in one individual is unrealistic, it is not that far from the aspirations of many modern women. Rampant consumerism is partly to blame as more and more commodities are seen as 'must-haves'. Rising prices and society's expectations that children should be given experiences and sport and music lessons augment the pressure to earn. Many are trapped in the grip of trying to be super-woman: the perfect mother, wife, housekeeper and earner.

The one glaring omission from this list of accomplishments is spending time worshipping God. Without his strength, none of this is possible.

Lord, forgive me when I compare myself to others and strive to be everything. And forgive me when I allow others' expectations to restrict my aspirations and limit my growth.

MICHELE D. MORRISON

Words of wisdom

**She speaks with wisdom, and faithful instruction is on her tongue...
The wisdom that comes from heaven is first of all pure; then peace-loving, considerate, submissive, full of mercy and good fruit, impartial
and sincere. (NIV)**

Wise words require discernment and self-control; it is so easy to blurt out
an unconsidered opinion but such outbursts need reining in. I often think
of Mary, Jesus' mother, of whom it is written that she pondered things in
her heart. In other words, she chewed things over with God before she
spoke, and I would imagine that the result was she often held her peace.

Wise words promote peace, not dissension. They build up and don't
tear down. They reflect and give glory to God, speaking justice and mercy
and love. And their fruit is sweet to the taste and enriches life, growing the
kingdom.

Wisdom and understanding, according to James, are revealed by leading a good and humble life, devoid of envy and selfish ambition. It seems
that this inspiring woman worked away diligently without comparing
herself to others. Such perfection as she embodies is more likely to excite
envy than to inspire people to imitate it. Focusing on the tasks God has
called you to do and working at them with all your might prevents envy,
lazy thinking and a loose tongue.

Anne is a dear friend who was once my Sunday school teacher. She
is 95 and lives in the same residence as my mother. Having sustained a
couple of bone-breaks through falls, she moved into this place before
my mother did. When I asked her how she liked living there, she thought
a moment, and then she said, 'I'm content.' Although Anne misses her
home where she raised her family, and the independence of having a car,
she has assessed her situation prayerfully and accepted her limitations.

To my mind, contentment is a sign of wisdom. Gone is all striving, all
envy and selfish ambition. May I remember this in my old age.

---

*Father God, impart in me wisdom from above, and help me to hold my
tongue unless I have something positive and encouraging to say.*

MICHELE D. MORRISON

Busy fingers

She sets about her work vigorously; her arms are strong for her tasks. She sees that her trading is profitable, and her lamp does not go out at night. (NIV)

As already noted, the activities in this chapter are not a prescriptive list of chores, but offer a broad sweep of some of the God-endorsed possibilities open to women. Here there is a hint at a level of physical fitness displayed in vigour and strength. If we're going to stay on track for the work we do, we need to keep fit.

Women have often been, and still often are, victims of discrimination, treated as second-class citizens. Societal expectations and even, tragically, church rules can limit the possibilities open to women. But I know many women flourishing in the work options described in this chapter.

Creative homemaking: Adrienne is gifted at interior design and creates a home both welcoming and beautiful. Managing import-export business: Sheena trades in textiles from India, visiting factories and arranging the shipment of orders. Diligent food prep: Mhairi is careful in sourcing food without harmful additives and ensuring a steady supply of fresh produce is available in her home. Skilful farming and land management: Morag raises sheep and shows and sells them at market. Spinning and weaving: Belinda is a silk weaver, teaching classes and creating items of beauty and grace. Astute financial planning: Pauline uses her skills to run debt counselling courses.

The picture here is not of an overburdened working wife and mother juggling an outside job and sinking, exhausted, into bed every night. Instead, it is of an energetic, enthusiastic woman who is well educated in the ways of the world as well as the demands of the home and who, I believe, chooses her own path.

Lord God, we pray for our sisters who live in homes or societies where they are discouraged from developing their God-given gifts. Encourage them, we pray.

MICHELE D. MORRISON

Fear-of-the-Lord sandwich

Charm can mislead and beauty soon fades. The woman to be admired and praised is the woman who lives in the Fear-of-God. (MSG)

The book of Proverbs champions wisdom and opens with the declaration that 'the fear of the Lord is the beginning of knowledge'. It closes with praise for a woman who fears the Lord – a woman shown to be wise and skilled in all she does.

The book's opening statement in *The Message* reads: 'Start with God – the first step in learning is bowing down to God' (1:7). Closing as it does with today's text, the message of Proverbs is that only God is reliable because everything else changes or deceives.

Fear is an unpleasant concept. The Bible quotes God or angels exhorting humans not to be afraid 366 times, so isn't it odd that God would then promote the fear of the Lord? As an ordinary believer trying to make sense of her Bible, I see a clear relationship between God's command to us not to be afraid of circumstances, angels, challenges, lack of provision, and so on, and his call to live in the fear of the Lord. When we live in the fear of the Lord, we have nothing else to fear and we can experience life in all its fullness. It seems that the 'meaty filling' of a life well lived is contained within the 'bread' of the fear of the Lord.

I had a great dad, full of love, fun and encouragement. I feared disappointing him, right up until he died at the age of 87. He was my dad, and I wanted to please him, not to pain him. Similarly, I think the fear of the Lord springs from our love for him, and our desire not to disappoint.

The Lord loves us so much. Women and men: we are made in his image; we are made to be his daughters and sons.

Lord, open up this phrase for me today. Teach me how to fear you. I want to live life well; I want to please you. You are my first priority. Show me how to do it, in Jesus' name.

MICHELE D. MORRISON

Hope at Advent

Lyndall Bywater writes:

I remember being invited to an Advent party a few years ago. The hosts had lived in Germany, a country which has a much stronger concept of Advent than we do in the UK, and the event consisted of plenty of stillness and silence, along with plenty of opportunities to consume delicious seasonal goodies. I found it a deeply moving experience, because it seemed to hold a lot of things in tension. There was a sense of anticipation for the coming season of Christmas, but there was also a sober note, as we faced up to the pain and sorrow which still touches our world.

As I sat there in the candlelight, I found myself musing on how easy it is to lose track of Advent altogether. Either we sail into Christmas weeks ahead of the day itself, simply because we want to mark the season with so many people in so many different ways: at school with the children, at work with our colleagues, at concerts, at carol-singing events and at church with all those who'll have gone away by the time the 25th comes around. Or alternatively, we take a Scrooge-like 'bah-humbug' approach, burying our heads in the sand until we really can't put the whole thing off any longer.

Advent is about holding the tension. Christ is coming, but he has not yet come; joy is dawning, but the night-time of grief is still very real; we anticipate, but still we wait. What better time of year, then, to explore the subject of hope. We Christians so often do to hope what we do to Christmas: either we over-emphasise the positives of life, glossing over the pain of what is still unresolved, or we plant ourselves firmly in the pessimist camp, not daring to hope for anything, because then life won't be able to disappoint us. But the Bible teaches that real hope is the balancing place between the future which we look towards, and the present which we live. Hope isn't afraid to acknowledge the mess we're in, but it firmly believes in a day when everything in this universe will be turned the right way up.

What does it mean to live in hope, and to bring hope into the lives of those around us? I trust you'll find much to encourage you as we explore the theme of hope together.

Living in the tension

Every warrior's boot used in battle and every garment rolled in blood will be destined for burning, will be fuel for the fire. (NIV)

> I see the world being slowly transformed into a wilderness; I hear the approaching thunder that, one day, will destroy us too. I feel the suffering of millions. And yet, when I look up at the sky, I somehow feel that everything will change for the better, that this cruelty too shall end, that peace and tranquillity will return once more.
> **Anne Frank**

Anne Frank and her family spent years in hiding during World War II, and her diary has become world-famous. Perhaps it's quotations like this that have so captured people's imagination over the years. Anne was scrupulously honest about what it meant to live in the midst of war, and yet there was a spark of hope in her which never seemed to get extinguished.

I find today's reading one of the most atmospheric in the Bible. Of course, I love that beautiful description of Jesus which rings out across the ages, but it is the verses before it which catch my imagination. It's as though the prophet was writing from the middle of an army encampment – a bit like an embedded journalist – staring into the bonfire, smelling the horrendous stench of battle, yet all the while imagining a day when that same bonfire could be used to burn up every terrible tool of war.

To have hope is not to gloss over our problems and pretend everything is fine. Whether life feels like a war zone at the moment or not, we all live in the tension between what we hope for and the reality of what we live. To have hope is to speak honestly of pain and fear, yet also to speak of a new, better day. To have hope is to sit in the middle of a battlefield and to speak of a Messiah.

As you go through the day, notice what it's like to live in the tension: bring the pains and frustrations to God in prayer, and remind yourself to look up and look for glimmers of hope on the horizon.

LYNDALL BYWATER

What exactly is hope?

And again, Isaiah says, 'The Root of Jesse will spring up, one who will arise to rule over the nations; in him the Gentiles will hope.' (NIV)

You probably know the story of the Sunday school teacher who planned a fun animal guessing-game for the children in her charge. As she started her spirited description of a small, furry, tree-dwelling creature with a bushy tail, a hand went up. Below the hand was the sullen face of an eight-year-old girl who clearly felt she had endured one too many silly Sunday school quizzes in her short little life.

'I know the answer is probably meant to be *Jesus*,' she said, 'but it sounds a lot like a squirrel to me.'

If we're going to study hope, then we should get something straight right at the beginning. We need to know what hope actually is; we need to distinguish it from all the fake versions doing the rounds. Is hope a kind of fairy-tale wishful thinking? Is it a manic conviction that everything will be fine… somehow? Is it all about being a 'glass half full' person who always thinks positively and believes the best?

As the world-weary eight-year-old in that Sunday school had already learnt, the answer to almost every question anyone ever asks about the Christian faith is 'Jesus', and today's question is no different. In Romans 15, Paul is rounding out one of the most spectacular theology lectures of the early church, and he's coming in to land with his core message: there is hope because there is Jesus. We can live well alongside one another and we can stand tall in this broken, shaken world of ours, because one has come who is, quite literally, the hope of the nations.

Hope isn't an attitude of mind. Hope is the God who became man and the man who is God. If you have him in your life, then you have hope.

May the God of hope fill you with all joy and peace as you trust in him, so that you may overflow with hope – so that you may overflow with Jesus – by the power of the Holy Spirit.

LYNDALL BYWATER

Who has the final word?

In you, Lord my God, I put my trust. I trust in you; do not let me be put to shame… No one who hopes in you will ever be put to shame. (NIV)

If you've ever been a rail commuter, then you'll know the cast-iron rule that, where there's a packed train about to depart, there's usually an empty one just behind it, going in exactly the same direction. You can tell the seasoned commuters on a platform because they're the ones who hang back from the scrum, in the confident belief that the journey home will be far more comfortable if they just wait a little longer.

Psalm 25 reads differently in different versions of the Bible, largely because translators have had to choose between the English words 'hope' and 'wait'. The Hebrew word means both. So, today's passage is either an exhortation to hope in the Lord, or it's an exhortation to wait for him. Put like that, it gives hope a different slant. We seasoned commuters aren't just vaguely wishing that an empty train might arrive. We are waiting in the confident assurance that one will definitely turn up soon.

When writing this psalm, David is in a low place. He's been betrayed by his friends, his sins have caught up with him and his enemies are winning. He could give up, or he could try to manufacture some human solutions, but he is set on one thing and one thing only: to wait for God. He may have sinned, but he won't let his shame have the last word. He may have been betrayed, but he won't let vengeance have the last word. He may be losing the battle, but he won't let despair have the last word. The only one who gets to have the last word in his life is God.

To hope in God is to wait for him; things may look hopeless, but darkness does not have to have the last word. Hope is on the way.

Have you got tired of waiting? Are you tempted to give up, or to try and find a human fix? Ask God to renew your patience today, and to reassure you that he has things in hand.

LYNDALL BYWATER

What price hope?

We also glory in our sufferings, because we know that suffering produces perseverance; perseverance, character; and character, hope. (NIV)

One of the first things I do when I'm preparing a set of Bible notes is to put my theme-word into the search bar of my Bible app. You can imagine my surprise when, having typed the word 'hope' into the little box, the Bible book which came up as having the largest number of references to hope in it was the book of Job. I actually laughed out loud! 1,070 occurrences of the word 'hope' in a book about a man who experienced terrible suffering! The next result was the book of Psalms, with a measly 34 instances of the word.

It turns out on further inspection that 'hope' doesn't appear 1,070 times in Job. It's just that someone has associated every single verse in the book with that particular theme-word. I was about to ping off a stern message to the app developer when I suddenly stopped in my tracks, because maybe that's not such a crazy idea after all.

Paul teaches the Romans an uncomfortable little recipe for hope. It starts with suffering, which gets hard-boiled into character, and character in turn infuses us with hope. The word Paul uses for 'character' is an unusual one, and it implies something which is proven, reliable or solid. Like metal when it's tempered or muscle when it's thickened, character is the strong, solid core which holds us up and keeps us going, through the most difficult times of life. To grow that kind of character, we need to persevere through the suffering. That doesn't mean we have to enjoy it or paste on a veneer of fake cheerfulness. It just means we lean on God and keep going forward. And in that place of costly trust, you may be surprised to discover an indomitable kind of hope springing up.

What does character look like for you today? Is there a bit of teeth-gritting to be done, as you face something you'd rather avoid? Be honest with God about your feelings, and ask him to give you courage.

LYNDALL BYWATER

Hope uprooted

He has blocked my way so I cannot pass; he has shrouded my paths in darkness… He tears me down on every side till I am gone; he uproots my hope like a tree. (NIV)

The question 'How are you?' sends me into a tailspin at the moment. The answer is that I am grieving, seeking direction, feeling confused and bubbling with hope. The trouble is, that's a long answer to give, and I still can't do it without crying. The hope is more irrepressible than ever, but the grief is still sharp.

Yesterday, I mentioned my amusement at discovering that my Bible app shows 1,070 references to hope in the book of Job, so today I thought we'd better explore how this beleaguered man managed to find hope in the midst of his desperate circumstances. For the first half of chapter 19, Job is more hopeless than hopeful, and he's blaming God. Not only has God not given him any reason to hope, but God has actively uprooted the hope he did have.

Having spent years trying to get pregnant, this is a sentiment I well understand. I had hopes of becoming a mum, and it's confusing and heartbreaking to feel that God has taken some of my most precious hopes and dreams and pulled them up by the roots. That's a bleak place to be.

And yet, by the end of the chapter, Job is singing a hymn of hope. Whatever dreams he may have harboured for living a successful life have now been replaced with the astonishing confidence that he will one day encounter God himself. God may have uprooted Job's own hopes, but he plants some stronger, sturdier ones in their place. There's simply no guarantee that we will have all our own life-dreams fulfilled, but if we hang on in there with God, evergreen hope will start to spring up in us – the sort of hope we could never conjure up in ourselves; the sort of hope that never dies.

Are you grieving for some uprooted hopes today? Perhaps you tended them for years, and it feels as though God has cruelly torn them down. Ask him to fill the cracks in your soul with his miraculous, never-fading hope.

LYNDALL BYWATER

Hope enlarged

But those who hope in the Lord will renew their strength. They will soar on wings like eagles; they will run and not grow weary, they will walk and not be faint. (NIV)

Somewhere in the middle of a long journey through fertility treatment, I turned 40. About six months before the big day, God stopped me in my tracks, and suggested I might like to take a break from the gruelling round of procedures, drugs, diets, supplements and scans, so that I could celebrate this milestone birthday with gusto. I was suspicious. Was this his roundabout way of telling me to give up on my dreams? Was he thinking I cared more about a set of numbers on my birth certificate than about having a child? It turned out that the answer to both questions was 'no'. He just knew I needed a break, and he wanted me to celebrate me – the big picture of my life and all that he had given me.

When you're hoping for something, it's easy to become a single-issue person, focusing all your energy on that one goal, and viewing anything else as a distraction. The trouble is, that's a dangerous and exhausting track to be on. When we hope 'in the Lord', he refuses to let us lose sight of the bigger picture. This Isaiah prophecy is written to a people in exile, and they had probably become rather 'single-issue' about the need to get back to the land God had promised them. Yet God's words enlarge their focus. Their single issue may not yet be resolved, but it is only one wrinkle in the vast, beautiful tapestry of his creative goodness.

After a splendid month or two of birthday celebrations, God brought me back to the fertility treatment, refreshed and restored. He doesn't forget; he doesn't dismiss our dreams; but he does sometimes ask us to step back and let him show us the bigger picture. Only then can he renew our strength.

Have you been pursuing something you long for? Is God asking you to ease up and step back for a while? Why not make this festive season a time of celebration and renewal? Let him show you his bigger picture.

LYNDALL BYWATER

You can't earn hope

When life is heavy and hard to take, go off by yourself. Enter the silence. Bow in prayer. Don't ask questions: wait for hope to appear. Don't run from trouble. Take it full-face. The 'worst' is never the worst. (MSG)

Did your parents have ways of inspiring you to good behaviour when you were young? Rumours of an increase in pocket money, perhaps, or the promise of a favourite treat? We learn from a very young age that good behaviour produces rewards, and that bad behaviour doesn't. It's an important foundational lesson for helping us to become morally responsible human beings, but it has a sting in the tail – one which many parents fail to remove, and one which can truly hamper our ability to trust God. You see, if a child learns that good things happen when they do well, it is a small step to believing that if bad things happen, it must be because they have done badly and are being punished.

   Today's reading is rather a rollercoaster. Jeremiah seems to see-saw between complaint and praise, despair and hope. One minute he's bemoaning the dreadful state of his existence, and the next he's revelling in God's goodness. The contrast is almost jarring. In our own tough times, it's all too easy for that age-old reward/punishment lesson to surface, telling us that bad things are happening because we've done something wrong and God is displeased with us. Our pain and sorrow are often accompanied by a feeling that he is distant. Yet Jeremiah isn't bound by that way of thinking. He feels every bitter drop of pain, and at the same time he senses the nearness and the goodness of God. The two aren't mutually exclusive. He knows he isn't perfect, but he knows he's loved by an eternally compassionate Father.

   We can't earn hope. All the earning was done by Jesus at the cross. Hope isn't a reward for good behaviour, and hopelessness isn't a punishment for bad behaviour. Hope is yours today because you are his.

Has a feeling of hopelessness seemed like God's way of saying he's not pleased with you? If so, ask him to help you shake off that lie. Tough times come and go, but God's unconditional love for you never changes.

LYNDALL BYWATER

Hope unforeseen

When Joseph woke up, he did what the angel of the Lord had commanded him and took Mary home as his wife. (NIV)

One of the perks of having been married for 18 years is that we occasionally get asked to help other people prepare for marriage. It's a great privilege, and it always involves asking couples about their hopes for the future. At this time of year, I can't help wondering what it would have been like to do 'marriage prep' with Mary and Joseph. I'm guessing that, had anyone asked them what they hoped for their future, neither of them would have said, 'We plan to parent the child who will be God incarnate, sent to save his people from their sins.'

We don't know much about either of them, but what we do read in the Bible is enough to tell us that they were humble, gentle people, full of kindness and integrity. I imagine they fully intended to work hard, to parent well and to be upstanding members of their local community. Yet the future God had in store for them was far above and beyond any plans they'd made for themselves. Perhaps there were dark moments when they wished they hadn't been chosen for this most remarkable of parenting assignments, but they embraced it anyway, and they are remembered for it over two millennia later.

When you walk with the creator of the universe, future planning becomes an altogether more unpredictable business. It's good to set your sights on where you want to go, but you always have to remember that he may have a wholly different plan in mind. He is endlessly good and he will never force his will upon you, but I reckon Mary and Joseph would tell you to put your trust in him, because his hopes and dreams for you will always be a million times more fulfilling than anything you could ever have planned for yourself.

"'I belong to the Lord, body and soul," replied Mary. "Let it happen as you say"' (Luke 1:38, JBP). Can you echo her prayer today?

LYNDALL BYWATER

Living up to hope

Love others well, and don't hide behind a mask; love authentically. Despise evil; pursue what is good as if your life depends on it… Do not forget to rejoice, for hope is always just around the corner. (Voice)

No matter where you live, there's a high chance you'll have seen or heard a Salvation Army band playing carols in the streets recently. I grew up in the Salvation Army, and making joyful music has been part of our history since the earliest days of the movement. As with many traditions, though, we have occasionally been guilty of missing the point. One particular song, written in the late 1800s by one of the Salvation Army's early fire-brands, starts with the words 'Joy, joy, joy, there is joy in the Salvation Army!'

Trust me – few congregations could have made those words sound as dreary and dirge-like as we did, in the church where I grew up. Had you heard us singing them, joy would have been furthest from your mind.

In verse 12, Paul says 'Be joyful in hope' (NIV). Paul's letter to the Romans is riddled with this joyful hope. The first eleven chapters are a superb thesis on why we have every reason to live in hope.

Then, in chapter 12, his tone changes, and he spends the last quarter of the book grounding that theology in practical advice. Why? Because hope cannot be transmitted if it remains just a theory. I can devise the most convincing intellectual arguments for why I have hope, but those arguments are unlikely to ever inspire hope in anyone else. For hope to be transmitted, it needs to be lived out in practical ways.

Over the coming days, we'll examine what hope looks like when it's fleshed out in real life, but for today, let's start where Paul starts: hope loves joyfully. If you tell someone there's hope, then load them down with criticism and negativity, all they'll feel is hopeless. If you lavish a smile and some encouragement on them, they're highly likely to blossom into hope.

Lord Jesus, you are hope incarnate. In your words and your deeds, you set captives free from prisons of hopelessness. Teach me to be someone who doesn't just talk hope, but who lives it, too.

LYNDALL BYWATER

Tell your hope story

The day for building your walls will come, the day for extending your boundaries. (NIV)

> If one man can destroy everything, why can't one girl change it?
> **Malala Yousafzai**

Malala Yousafzai was only a child when she started changing the world. She decided to campaign for girls in her home country of Pakistan to have equal rights to education, a stance which resulted in the Taliban issuing a death threat against her. In 2012, when she was just 15, a gunman acted on that threat, shooting her in the head. She survived, and she's been speaking out for justice ever since.

Thousands of years before Malala was born, the prophet Micah was doing his bit to change things. We don't know much of his story, but today's passage suggests that he himself had been through tough times. He had found God to be a faithful rescuer, and he wanted to carry that message of hope to his people. His account is honest: he brought darkness on himself through his own sin, but God reached down and drew him back to light and healing. If God could do that for him, then he could surely bring Israel out of their destructive patterns of sin, to a season of restoration and rebuilding.

Our world needs people like Micah and Malala: people who have come through darkness and still have hope. Amidst the confusion of global politics and the turmoil of terrorism and natural disasters, people badly need to hear that darkness doesn't have to have the last word, that redemption is possible for this broken world. They need to hear the stories of those who've faced darkness and come through to light. Your life may not seem as heroic as Malala's, nor your words as poetic as Micah's, but never underestimate the power of your story to spark hope in the hearts of those who hear it.

Think about your own story for a few moments. Where have you seen God's hand at work, bringing you through darkness into light? Where have you seen hope? Now, who could you tell that story to today?

LYNDALL BYWATER

Deal with despair

He has sent me to bind up the broken-hearted… to bestow on them a crown of beauty instead of ashes, the oil of joy instead of mourning, and a garment of praise instead of a spirit of despair. (NIV)

The *Oxford English Dictionary* defines despair as 'a complete loss or absence of hope', and the *Cambridge English Dictionary* goes on to add that it is 'the feeling that there is no hope and that you can do nothing to improve a difficult or worrying situation'.

If we're going to talk about hope, we must also talk about despair. If hope is part of the kingdom Jesus came to bring, then it stands to reason that the enemy would have a strategy to oppose it, and that strategy is despair. The absence of hope isn't a neutral state; it's a dark, cold place. If you've ever encountered despair, either in your own life or someone else's, you'll know just how potent it is.

It encourages me, then, to notice that getting rid of the 'spirit of despair' is one of the things Jesus promises to do, and since it's right up there alongside things like setting captives free and restoring sight to the blind, it must need a miracle.

For someone who has just started feeling a bit discouraged and weary, words of hope will help to fan their faith into flames again, but if despair has taken hold, then it's a supernatural intervention that's needed. If you've been trying to speak hope over someone who's in despair, and have been feeling more and more despairing yourself because you just can't get through, then take heart. You're not doing anything wrong; you're just waiting for a miracle.

When we face the impossible, we pray. So, each time you feel discouraged by the futility and toxicity of despair, stop and ask the Holy Spirit to knock a few bricks out of that wall of hopelessness. The results may not be instantaneous, but your prayer will be heard, used and answered.

Take some time to reflect on your own life, and on the lives of those you're supporting. Where do you see despair at work? Name it for what it is, and give it to God in prayer.

LYNDALL BYWATER

Try generosity

Give away your life; you'll find life given back, but not merely given back – given back with bonus and blessing. Giving, not getting, is the way. Generosity begets generosity. (MSG)

Like most teenagers, I had strong opinions about my parents' shortcomings. They didn't have many, but one of the ones which annoyed me most was their tendency to try to have conversations with me before 9.00 am. They would come in to my room on their way out to work, with a view to making plans or asking complicated questions. Suffice it to say, I did my best to derail their early-morning positivity with a healthy dose of: 'I can't. It'll never work. What's the point? I don't care.'

I suspect my parents sometimes got exasperated, but fortunately they are people who love Jesus, and so they would have taken seriously his injunctions in today's passage to be kind and patient, despite my lack of cooperation. The truth is, even when we're not teenagers any more, we humans have a propensity to negativity. We're all too good at seeing the many reasons why things won't work out. But hope cannot coexist with negativity. Hope goes against the grain. Hope always thinks positively.

On other mornings, my parents would come in and tell me they'd done something nice for me, or bought me something I really wanted. Funnily enough, on those mornings, I was far more willing to engage in conversation. On those mornings, anything was possible. Teenagers are simple souls, and I was living out the eternal truth that generosity has a knack of short-circuiting our negativity.

When someone surprises you with something good, it rewires your brain, even just for a moment, and that can be enough to ignite hope again.

Jesus has a radical message. Where a critical, negative attitude is sapping hope, don't join the pity party. Instead, deploy a bit of generosity. You'll be amazed at how it can surprise people back into hope again.

Are you feeling infuriated by someone who's stuck in negativity? Ask God to show you something generous you could do for them. It's not your job to change their mindset, but your kindness might lead them back to hope.

LYNDALL BYWATER

Lend your hope

Let us hold unswervingly to the hope we profess, for he who promised is faithful. And let us consider how we may spur one another on towards love and good deeds. (NIV)

My favourite scene in Tolkien's *The Lord of the Rings* appears near the beginning of the story. Frodo is just starting to get his head around the enormity of the task before him, when he suddenly finds himself surrounded by friends who want to accompany him on his quest. Just as he is getting used to the idea of the lone hero, his friends pile in to rid him of any such foolish notions. The hobbit Merry simply says, 'You can trust us to stick to you through thick and thin – to the bitter end… but you cannot trust us to let you face trouble alone.'

Even Frodo has to admit that the adventure looks altogether more doable with such determined allies at his side.

The latter part of today's reading is perhaps one of the most famous passages about hope in the New Testament, yet we are rather prone to forgetting that it is written in the plural, not the singular. The writer isn't exhorting me to hold on to the hope that I profess. It's something 'we' do – all of us together, giving each other courage and spurring each other on. Hope grows when we show up for one another.

It's all too easy to get into a problem-solving mentality when it comes to hope. We think that, to bring hope to those around us, we need to be good at making people feel better or finding solutions to their problems, but that's a wrong notion, and an exhausting one at that. You may have no idea how to change things for someone, but that doesn't mean you can't offer them hope. Promise to stand with them – to walk with them through the joys and the challenges, and you will help make the road ahead seem brighter.

Father God, forgive me when I close my eyes and fail to look out for my fellow travellers. Help me today to look for opportunities to lend the hand of hope to those around me.

LYNDALL BYWATER

Hope incarnate; hope in you

What was hidden for ages, generations and generations, is now being revealed to his holy ones… The glorious riches of this mystery is the indwelling of the Anointed in you! (Voice)

With just four days to go till Christmas, how is your 'hope-ometer'? Are you hopeful that all the shopping will get finished, the presents will get wrapped, friends and family will all be in the right place at the right time, and everyone will have fun? Or are you busy praying that despair doesn't get a grip of you, as you navigate the 101 things you still need to do?

Whatever your state of mind, my hope and prayer for you is that you won't forget to have your own celebration, come 25 December. You see, this chapter in Paul's letter to the Colossians reveals an astonishing truth about Jesus coming into our world – one which most of us forget, especially amidst the hectic rush of a busy Christmas. Paul says that the whole point of God becoming human and walking our earth was that he would one day, by his Spirit, make his home in us.

Yes – the birth in the stable, the 33 years of life, the three remarkable years of ministry and the history-tilting death and resurrection were all absolutely crucial, but the endgame, the point of it all, was that he would take up residence in us. Even God, the creator of the universe, never planned to do it all on his own. He fully intended to draw us round him, a family bearing his name, filled with his hope, transforming the world with his love.

Christmas is a time for joining with others in the celebration of Jesus' birth, but it should also be a deeply intimate moment of reconsecration for you and the one who has won your heart. After all, part of God's genius plan for bringing the hope of glory to this world is 'Christ in you'.

Is there a piece of jewellery or clothing you could wear on Christmas Day, as a reminder of your relationship with Jesus? Take time to look into his face and remember that he came to be God with you, God in you.

LYNDALL BYWATER

Journeys of faith

Jean Watson writes:

All our journeys of faith on earth are within the context of the Big Journey – the one from earth to heaven, from this life to the next.

In this series, we will be looking at: some journeys of faith involving Mary, Joseph and Elizabeth; the disciples on the Emmaus road and our journey into the new year; the big sweeping journey of faith by the people of Israel from Egypt to Canaan; the utterly off-the-scale journey of faith by Jesus from heaven to earth, from eternity to here; and our overall journey of faith from earth to heaven, from here to eternity.

Here's a poem about our overall journey – our pilgrim's progress, if you like. Which of the experiences highlighted can you empathise with? As you go through this series of journeys of faith, I hope you will be able to identify with many of the experiences of those involved and find help and inspiration for yourself in your daily walk of faith with Jesus.

> It all seemed easy, clear as day;
> I ticked the box and said the prayer,
> and off I went on the king's highway.
> But then the road was sometimes rough
> and sometimes steep and through the dark.
> My strength alone was not enough.
> 'Where are you now, my Lord and friend?'
> Only the silence makes reply.
> Driven to deeper listening, then
> I hear a whispered, 'Here am I.
> Beloved, take my strength, my hand.'
> And when I do I seem to spy
> some friends around, a light ahead
> and rest to come and nourishment,
> and on I press with lighter tread.
> There may be dangers, miles to go,
> but still the way's the only way
> that takes his pilgrims safely home.

Abraham to Jesus

Fellow children of Abraham and you God-fearing Gentiles, it is to us that this message of salvation has been sent. (NIV)

Have you ever been on a 'Bible overview' course? Getting a sight of the bigger picture as the context for your own journey of faith can be exhilarating. We obviously can't attempt such an overview here, but in our passage, Paul summarises a big slice of the story of God's plan of salvation for the world from Abraham to Jesus. We could go even further back and say God's plan of salvation started with God's creation of the universe and later on included his choice of Abraham and his descendants to be the means by which he would rescue, save and restore his creation, which was no longer 'very good' (Genesis 1:31).

Notice the important milestones that Paul picks out when he is outlining the journey of faith involving Abraham and sweeping on to Jesus:

- the exile in Egypt from which God delivered his people
- the long, circuitous journey to Canaan, the promised land
- the rule under first judges, then kings
- in particular and crucially the rule of King David, from whose line Jesus was born, the Messiah, God's Son
- Jesus' life on earth and his death and resurrection.

Resulting from this, salvation – forgiveness and a restored relationship with God, and a new way of living and being – became available to all.

This Abraham-to-Jesus summary highlights a tremendous sweeping journey of faith, involving many different people and events.

It's a journey that's still going on as people like us choose to join in by accepting the salvation that God offers through Jesus by his Holy Spirit. As Paul writes in Ephesians 2:8–9: 'It is by grace you have been saved, through faith – and this is not from yourselves, it is the gift of God – not by works, so that no one can boast.'

Is getting on the salvation track all that needs to happen in anyone's journey of faith? 2 Peter 1:5–9, Ephesians 2:10 and James 2:17, for example, may help us to answer that question. Pray through your response to this.

JEAN WATSON

Mary to Elizabeth

Mary got ready and hurried to a town in the hill country of Judea, where she entered Zechariah's home and greeted Elizabeth. (NIV)

Back story: Mary is a very young girl living in Nazareth. She is engaged to Joseph, a descendant of King David and newly pregnant – but not by him – after a life-changing encounter with a messenger and a message from God. Elizabeth is a much older relative of Mary's, possibly a cousin, married to a priest, Zechariah, and living somewhere in the hill country of Judea. Until recently, she was childless, but is now amazingly six months' pregnant.

Can you imagine Mary's feelings as she travelled to Elizabeth, desperately hoping that she, of all people, would understand what she was about to tell her? She was travelling the four- or five-day journey in faith – certainly; but lots of other emotions and thoughts must have been involved as well. Awe and excitement vying, perhaps, with incredility, shock and apprehension. 'Was that real – an angel and that message? Were they really for me? What'll happen now? Will anyone believe me?' We don't know if Joseph had had his message from God before Mary visited Elizabeth but, if he hadn't, she must have been worried about his and everyone else's reaction.

But, on her arrival, there was massive reassurance. Elizabeth welcomed her with open arms and blessing. 'Why should I be so fortunate as to have the mother of my Lord coming to me?' she exclaimed. Mary now had a fuller picture of the child she was to bear. The angel had told her that he would be the Son of the most high with an everlasting kingdom; now Elizabeth spoke of him as Lord, the name given to God. So here were two women, chosen by God for unique unprecedented roles in his plans, sharing secrets that would rock the universe! It caused Mary to burst into song. You might like to note what specifically and particularly she was thrilled about (Luke 1:36–55).

In a smaller way, has God ever surprised and delighted you in your journey of faith? Did you sing a song/write a prayer of praise to him, or could you perhaps do that in your own way now?

JEAN WATSON

Mary and Joseph to Bethlehem

[Joseph] went there to register with Mary, who was pledged to be married to him and was expecting a child. (NIV)

What turbulence Joseph had experienced in his life! Betrothed to a woman who was expecting a child that was not his, he must have been devastated – until God, in a dream, gave him some staggering information and told him to marry Mary but have no sexual relations with her until her son had been born. That Joseph understood and obeyed showed amazing faith.

Months later, he had to come down to earth with a bang. The Roman authorities were issuing orders in relation to a census and taxation. This meant that Joseph would have to travel the three- or four-day journey from Nazareth to Bethlehem with his heavily pregnant wife, Mary.

Being the people they were and after having had such amazing spiritual encounters, Mary and Joseph surely travelled in faith. But it was likely faith tested by weariness, uncertainty and anxiety, both on the road and when they were offered poor, makeshift accommodation – perhaps a cave used as a stable. There Mary's son was born, wrapped in strips of cloth and placed in a manger, an animal's feeding trough.

Please reread the story with these two questions in mind:

- Who, imaginatively, are you in this story? In other words: who do you identify with and feel with and for in this story?
- Why did God allow his Son to be born in that way? (Think of Jesus' priorities in his ministry and how the manner of his birth might have hinted at this. It might help you to look up Matthew 11:4–5; Luke 22:24–27.)

'O holy child of Bethlehem… be born in us today' ('O Little Town of Bethlehem', Phillips Brooks): how can the child of Bethlehem be born in us (you, me) today?

JEAN WATSON

The shepherds to Bethlehem

'Let's go to Bethlehem and see this thing that has happened, which the Lord has told us about.' (NIV)

Here's part of a poem I wrote inspired by the story in our passage for today. It imagines what it might have been like for a young lad to be with his father watching their sheep that night when the heavenly messengers appeared with their incredible message. The poem ends like this:

> *So it was he who heard them first –*
> *born on the gusting breeze*
> *down from the midnight sky and stars of gold –*
> *the earliest echoes of unearthly wings and songs*
> *heralding the shepherd that would come*
> *in time from out of it*
> *to carry the lost universe*
> *back safely to its fold.*

The shepherds on the hills above Bethlehem couldn't know the full implications of what the angels told them. But they heard the words 'Saviour', 'Christ' and 'Lord', so they certainly knew that God was doing something new and sensational. And wouldn't they also have been thrilled and amazed that *they* had been told? Out of everyone, it was they who had been chosen to be the early recipients of such important heavenly news! However, with the privilege of hindsight, we can see that what happened was completely in keeping with Jesus' ministry and his priorities.

The shepherds' response – 'Let's go and see' – followed by action showed their faith as they made the short journey to Bethlehem. But as well as faith, they must have journeyed with excitement and also some bemusement – for would this wonderful child really be born in an animal's trough? They had certainly encountered the God of surprises, as had also, recently, Elizabeth and Zechariah, and Mary and Joseph. Have you?

Reflect in God's presence on any or all of your encounters with the God of surprises as you have journeyed in faith.

JEAN WATSON

The wise men to Bethlehem

Magi from the east came to Jerusalem and asked, 'Where is the one who has been born king of the Jews? We saw his star when it rose and have come to worship him.' (NIV)

Christmas nativity plays usually have visits to baby Jesus in the stable from any number of shepherds and three wise man. But we don't know how many magi there were, only that they brought three gifts; and we do know that they arrived at a later date when Mary and Joseph were in a house and Jesus was a child (Matthew 2:11).

Think about why this journey of faith was so significant:

- The magi came to Bethlehem, the city of David and of David's greater Son: the Messiah.
- They were Gentiles from distant lands and yet God was calling them through signs in the heavens to worship Jesus.
- They realised that his kingship was of quite a different order to that of Herod or any other earthly ruler. The gift of gold that they offered him symbolised this unique kingship; frankincense symbolised divinity; and myrrh mortal man and/or perhaps sorrows and sadness.

Tremendous and persistent faith was required for this long journey. Did these magi or astrologers have ups and downs in their feelings as they travelled? It's not unlikely. But they continued to follow the guiding star all the way from the East – Persia, Babylon or Arabia, maybe – to Jerusalem and then, after conversations with different people and instructions from Herod, on to Bethlehem. There they knew with great joy that they had found the one they had come looking for – and, having worshipped and presented their gifts, they returned home as directed by God in a dream.

How can we relate to this story so far outside our ordinary experience? In our spiritual journey of faith, we can come to Jesus and give him, day by day, the gifts of our worship, our love, our commitment.

Where are you in your journey of faith today? Seeking and asking questions in Jerusalem? Or worshipping in Bethlehem?

JEAN WATSON

Escape to and from Egypt

An angel of the Lord appeared to Joseph in a dream. 'Get up,' he said, 'take the child and his mother and escape to Egypt.' (NIV)

To the Jews, Egypt was synonymous with exile: the place and situation from which God had delivered them and eventually brought them to a land of their own. That history prefigured what happened when the baby Jesus and his parents were 'exiled' in Egypt for a time and then returned to their own country.

Their journey to Egypt was made in faith: again, Joseph was spoken to by God in a dream and went with his family to Egypt as instructed, but it must have been a very worrying time and a huge upheaval. Moving is stressful at the best of times, but moving to a different country in great haste and fear must have tested Mary and Joseph's faith and peace of mind. But, despite all that, because of their faith and obedience, Jesus escaped the terrible fate of the babies still living in and around Bethlehem. Herod, ruthless and cruel and, following the visit and quest of the magi, paranoid about anyone who might threaten his power and position, ordered this terrible massacre.

The poignant prophecy about weeping and mourning refers to Rachel, Jacob's beloved wife, who died in childbirth on the way to Bethlehem.

God could have made Jesus invisible, or hidden him and his parents in some other miraculous way, but instead they had to escape to a place of safety just like 'ordinary' people! Of course, the escape and the return were under God's guidance, given in miraculous ways. In this unique time in the history of the universe, we see heaven meeting earth, the ordinary entwined with the extraordinary, reflecting the truth that this Jesus was both human and divine.

Reflect on a journey – actual, psychological, spiritual or some combination of those – that has tested your faith and obedience. How has that affected or now affects your relationship with yourself, others, God?

JEAN WATSON

From eternity to here

[Christ Jesus] being in very nature God, did not consider equality with God something to be used to his own advantage; rather, he made himself nothing by taking the very nature of a servant, being made in human likeness. (NIV)

We can grasp only faintly the stupendous journey of faith that Jesus took from heaven to earth. Father, Son and Holy Spirit were the amazing Trinity of perfect love and truth, joy and unity; the Son voluntarily left all that.

This is how *THE MESSAGE* paraphrases part of our passage:

He had equal status with God but didn't think so much of himself that he had to cling to the advantages of that status no matter what… He set aside the privileges of deity and took on the status of a slave… It was an incredibly humbling process. He didn't claim special privileges. Instead, he lived a selfless, obedient life and then died a selfless, obedient death – and the worst kind of death at that – a crucifixion.

After the journey from eternity to here, Jesus returned from here to eternity (v. 9). At the same time, as we know from other Bible passages, Jesus is still here with us through his Holy Spirit.

Our own journeys of faith can't match Christ's journey of faith from eternity to here. But can we follow his example and, through his Holy Spirit, develop something of the attitude and mindset he had as he undertook that momentous journey – the attitude of 'giving up his own rights' for the sake of us? Have you ever turned down a privilege or promising opportunity for the sake of a greater good for others? Perhaps you can think of friends who have done something like that. I know of people who, following the example of Christ's love and humility, have sold their big houses and moved into something smaller in a poorer neighbourhood for the sake of sharing and living out Christ's love and good news there.

Reflect on what putting the following verse into practice could look like – or has looked like – for you: 'Your attitude should be the same as that of Christ Jesus' (v. 5).

JEAN WATSON

From here to eternity

Surely your goodness and love will follow me all the days of my life, and I will dwell in the house of the Lord for ever. (NIV)

The psalmist uses the metaphor of sheep and their shepherd to describe the journey of faith from earth to heaven – from here to eternity. What terrain do the sheep and their shepherd travel through? What do they experience? There are green pastures and quiet waters, but there are also shadowed valleys where danger and death await. There are enemies, but there is also the shepherd who protects and feeds, refreshes and reassures his sheep. And, finally, there is the arrival at the eternal home.

In Bunyan's *Pilgrim's Progress*, the pilgrims experience a variety of ups and downs. They encounter people and situations that symbolise the world, the flesh and the devil – tempting them to turn aside from the right road. They also encounter enemies, including the most feared Apollyon; these enemies of God fight them, falsely accuse them, treat them violently and drive them to despair. But they are also rescued, refreshed, given good advice, helped to see where they went wrong, helped on their way by the prince and his friends and eventually welcomed into the eternal city.

> The settled happiness and security which we all desire God withholds from us by the very nature of the world: but joy, pleasure, merriment he has scattered broadcast… Our Father refreshes us on the journey with some pleasant inns, but will not encourage us to mistake them for home.
>
> C.S. Lewis, *The Business of Heaven*

We lodge in 'the shadowlands' – C.S. Lewis again. Perhaps you are enjoying sunshine, still waters and green pastures, or experiencing shadowed valleys and 'enemies'. Either way, we are 'the sheep of his pasture' and the good shepherd is with us all as we travel hopefully and then arrive to enjoy a life that is unimaginably full, rich and wonderful.

Share with God and perhaps a trusted friend where you are in your journey of faith right now so you can express your thankfulness, or your vulnerability and need of help.

JEAN WATSON

The road to Emmaus

Jesus himself came up and walked along with them. (NIV)

Today I want to focus on journeying into the new, particularly into the new year; but the same principles could apply to journeying into anything new – a new job, home, stage of life, role, health issue…

As you read through today's passage, can you identify the emotions and actions of the two disciples? Perhaps in your journey of faith into something new, you have felt and reacted as they did. Or were your emotions and actions completely different?

They were downcast and sad. Some of us feel like that in new situations; others may be excited and hopeful.

They couldn't make sense of what seemed to have happened. Feelings of bewilderment are not unusual at such times of momentous change.

They were willing to share their concerns with someone who came alongside, asked a question and showed interest. In their case, this turned out to be, as they later realised, Jesus.

Many have learnt the value of opening up to trusted people when their journey of faith seems bumpy and uncertain. At such times, it can be as though Jesus is speaking to us through them.

The two disciples were hospitable to this 'stranger' and were hugely blessed because of it. Being hospitable and receiving hospitality are great mutually beneficial blessings. See Hebrews 13:2 – but these disciples entertained more than angels: their guest was Jesus.

They had a eureka moment when things suddenly became clear: 'It's Jesus! He said he would rise again – and he has! We ought to have realised it earlier when he was talking to us and our hearts were strangely warmed. But now we see it and we can't keep quiet about it!' Spiritual 'eureka' moments are very special times when we suddenly grasp something precious and new, when Jesus seems very close and real on our journey of faith into the unknown future.

Pray for a closer walk with Jesus, and with others who are also walking with him, as you journey into the new year with its joys and challenges. May there be many special moments in 2019 when we experience Jesus more fully.

JEAN WATSON

Recommended reading

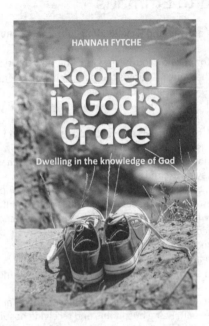

Sometimes it can be difficult to know where to start with getting to know God. Sure, we all know that the answer is to pray and read the Bible, but how and why? Starting from the truths we root ourselves in as Christians and how this motivates us to know God, *Rooted in God's Grace* discusses different rhythms we can use to connect with God and become like 'trees planted by water which send their roots out by the stream' (Jeremiah 17:7–8).

Rooted in God's Grace
Dwelling in the knowledge of God
Hannah Fytche
978 0 85746 587 0   £7.99
brfonline.org.uk

Anxious Times

Carmel Thomason

Foreword by Archbishop John Sentamu

A book of 24 undated reflections drawing on a range of relevant Bible passages to offer genuine hope and encouragement in anxious times. Encompassing the very human emotions of fear and anxiety, the reflections encourage us to draw comfort and strength from God's word even in those times when he seems silent to us. This book acknowledges that trust and hope in God's goodness doesn't always come easily, but when embraced we gain the strength to face our fear with courage and confidence.

Anxious Times
Carmel Thomason
978 0 85746 660 0 £3.99
brfonline.org.uk

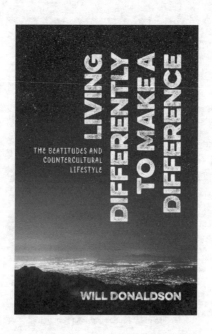

Few would doubt that we live in a wounded and broken world. But God has sent a Saviour, Jesus Christ, who calls us, in the beatitudes, to live an authentic, countercultural lifestyle. By being different we can make a difference, becoming the salt of the earth and the light of the world. Through living the beatitudes, we could make the world a better place.

Living Differently to Make a Difference
The beatitudes and countercultural lifestyle
Will Donaldson
978 0 85746 671 6 £7.99
brfonline.org.uk

To order

Online: **brfonline.org.uk**
Tel.: +44 (0)1865 319700
Mon–Fri 9.15–17.30

Delivery times within the UK are normally
15 working days. Prices are correct at the time of
going to press but may change without prior notice.

Title	Price	Qty	Total
Rooted in God's Grace	£7.99		
Anxious Times	£3.99		
Living Differently to Make a Difference	£7.99		

POSTAGE AND PACKING CHARGES			
Order value	UK	Europe	Rest of world
Under £7.00	£2.00	£5.00	£7.00
£7.00–£29.99	£3.00	£9.00	£15.00
£30.00 and over	FREE	£9.00 + 15% of order value	£15.00 + 20% of order value

Total value of books	
Postage and packing	
Total for this order	

Please complete in BLOCK CAPITALS

Title .... First name/initials .... Surname ....

Address ....

.... Postcode ....

Acc. No. .... Telephone ....

Email ....

Method of payment

❏ Cheque (made payable to BRF) ❏ MasterCard / Visa

Card no. ▢▢▢▢ ▢▢▢▢ ▢▢▢▢ ▢▢▢▢

Valid from ⅯⅯ ⅯⅯ ⅯⅯ Expires ⅯⅯ ⅯⅯ ⅯⅯ Security code* ▢▢▢

Last 3 digits on the reverse of the card

Signature* .... Date .... / .... / ....

*ESSENTIAL IN ORDER TO PROCESS YOUR ORDER

Please return this form with the appropriate payment to:

BRF, 15 The Chambers, Vineyard, Abingdon OX14 3FE | enquiries@brf.org.uk

To read our terms and find out about cancelling your order, please visit **brfonline.org.uk/terms**.

The Bible Reading Fellowship (BRF) is a Registered Charity (233280)

SUBSCRIPTION INFORMATION

Each issue of *Day by Day with God* is available from Christian bookshops everywhere. Copies may also be available through your church book agent or from the person who distributes Bible reading notes in your church.

Alternatively you may obtain *Day by Day with God* on subscription direct from the publishers. There are two kinds of subscription:

Individual subscriptions
covering 3 issues for 4 copies or less, payable in advance (including postage & packing).

To order, please complete the details on page 144 and return with the appropriate payment to: BRF, 15 The Chambers, Vineyard, Abingdon OX14 3FE

You can also use the form on page 144 to order a gift subscription for a friend.

Group subscriptions
covering 3 issues for 5 copies or more, sent to **one** UK address (post free).

Please note that the annual billing period for group subscriptions runs from 1 May to 30 April.

To order, please complete the details on page 143 and return with the appropriate payment to: BRF, 15 The Chambers, Vineyard, Abingdon OX14 3FE

You will receive an invoice with the first issue of notes.

All our Bible reading notes can be ordered online by visiting
biblereadingnotes.org.uk/subscriptions

For information about our other Bible reading notes,
and apps for iPhone and iPod touch, visit
biblereadingnotes.org.uk

All subscription enquiries should be directed to:
BRF, 15 The Chambers, Vineyard, Abingdon OX14 3FE
+44 (0)1865 319700 | enquiries@brf.org.uk

All our Bible reading notes can be ordered online by visiting
biblereadingnotes.org.uk/subscriptions

The group subscription rate for *Day by Day with God* will be £13.50 per person until April 2019.

☐ I would like to take out a group subscription for _____ (quantity) copies.

☐ Please start my order with the January 2019 / May 2019 / September 2019* issue.
I would like to pay annually/receive an invoice* with each edition of the notes.
(*delete as appropriate)

Please do not send any money with your order. Send your order to BRF and we will send you an invoice. The group subscription year is from 1 May to 30 April. If you start subscribing in the middle of a subscription year we will invoice you for the remaining number of issues left in that year.

Name and address of the person organising the group subscription:

Title _____ First name/initials _____ Surname _____

Address _____

_____ Postcode _____

Telephone _____ Email _____

Church _____

Name of Minister _____

Name and address of the person paying the invoice if the invoice needs to be sent directly to them:

Title _____ First name/initials _____ Surname _____

Address _____

_____ Postcode _____

Telephone _____ Email _____

Please return this form with the appropriate payment to:
BRF, 15 The Chambers, Vineyard, Abingdon OX14 3FE

To read our terms and find out about cancelling your order, please visit **brfonline.org.uk/terms**.

The Bible Reading Fellowship is a Registered Charity (233280)

DAY BY DAY WITH GOD INDIVIDUAL/GIFT SUBSCRIPTION FORM

To order online, please visit **biblereadingnotes.org.uk/subscriptions**

- [ ] I would like to give a gift subscription (please provide both names and addresses)
- [ ] I would like to take out a subscription myself (complete your name and address details only once)

Title _____ First name/initials _____ Surname _____

Address _____

_____ Postcode _____

Telephone _____ Email _____

Gift subscription name _____

Gift subscription address _____

_____ Postcode _____

Gift message (20 words max. or include your own gift card):

_____

_____

Please send *Day by Day with God* beginning with the January 2019 / May 2019 / September 2019 issue (*delete as appropriate*):

(please tick box)	UK	Europe	Rest of world
1-year subscription	[ ] £16.95	[ ] £25.20	[ ] £29.10
2-year subscription	[ ] £30.90	N/A	N/A

Total enclosed £ _____ (cheques should be made payable to 'BRF')

Please charge my MasterCard / Visa [ ] Debit card [ ] with £ _____

Card no. [ ][ ][ ][ ] [ ][ ][ ][ ] [ ][ ][ ][ ] [ ][ ][ ][ ]

Valid from [ ][ ] Expires [ ][ ] Security code* [ ][ ][ ]

Last 3 digits on the reverse of the card

Signature* _____ Date _____ / _____ / _____

*ESSENTIAL IN ORDER TO PROCESS YOUR ORDER

Please return this form with the appropriate payment to:
BRF, 15 The Chambers, Vineyard, Abingdon OX14 3FE

BRF

To read our terms and find out about cancelling your order, please visit **brfonline.org.uk/terms**.

The Bible Reading Fellowship is a Registered Charity (233280)

DBDWG0318